100 Years
of Women Police
in Australia

Tim Prenzler

AUSTRALIANACADEMICPRESS

First published 2015 by:
Australian Academic Press Group Pty. Ltd.
18 Victor Russell Drive
Samford Valley QLD 4520, Australia
www.australianacademicpress.com.au

National Library of Australia Cataloguing-in-Publication entry:

Creator: Prenzler, Tim, author
One Hundred Years of Women Police in Australia / Tim Prenzler.

ISBN   9781922117601 (paperback)
ISBN   9781922117618 (ebook)

Subjects: Policewomen--Australia--History.
 Sex role in the work environment--Australia.

Dewey Number: 363.20820994

Publisher: Stephen May

Copy Editor: Rhonda McPherson

Cover design: Maria Biaggini, The Letter Tree

Page design & typesetting: Australian Academic Press

Printing: Lightning Source

This book is dedicated to the memory of
Marie Sophie Prenzler (nee Johannes) 1861–1914
A reluctant pioneer

Norma Morris and Dulcie Bock, Queensland Police, 1947.

Contents

Preface

This book is the culmination of 25 years of research, starting when I began teaching Australian social issues, along with ethics and accountability, to police recruits at Griffith University in 1991. To my amazement, women made up one-third of classes. I was completely ignorant of the history of women in policing and a little unsure of women's ability to handle police work. Curiosity led to a meeting with Inspector Jill Bolen, who told me there was a dark history to gender relations in the Queensland Police — one that needed to be brought to light. I subsequently completed a Masters thesis on the Queensland experience, including the years of discrimination under Commissioner Terry Lewis, to which Jill Bolen was primarily referring. I later worked on a summary illustrated history of women in the Queensland Police with the Police Service's museum and the media unit.

As part of my Masters in Australian Studies, I also completed a summary history of women in Australian policing, and I went on to complete a number of discrete studies on specific aspects of gender relations in policing. These included studies of barriers to women in recruitment and the work of equity agencies. I have also conducted some international comparisons of the status of women police. More recently, I have been involved in research comparing the performance of male and female officers.

The world needs more women police — mainly because policing provides a relatively safe, secure, interesting and well-remunerated career path, and a source of economic independence and personal self-fulfilment for women. But also — at the risk of being labelled a 'gender essentialist' — we need more women police because communities need better policing services than those provided by men over the last 200 years. With that in mind, after charting the many complex processes by which formal gender equality was achieved in Australian policing, the book concludes with a simple recipe for eliminating discrimination and optimising the contributions of women to police work.

Over the years, I have received a great deal of assistance from numerous police officers, librarians, colleagues and research assistants. At the risk of offending those left out, I would like to make special mention of Jill Bolen, Christine Lidgard, Lisa Jones, David Gill, Rose Wintergreen-Arthur and Carol Ronken.

This book project was the subject of four unsuccessful applications to the Australian Research Council for modest funds for research assistance and travel to archives, state libraries, police academy libraries, and police unions in all the capital cities. In each case, the application was marked down by feminist scholars with various objections, including the wrong — but unspecified — theory. Thankfully, my employer at the time, Griffith University, provided sufficient funds for visits to these locations and collection of photocopied memos, letters, reports, and newspaper reports. (Much of this was in the days before that amazing online invention 'Trove'.) Together with several jurisdictionally based accounts, this has allowed me to piece together the main contours of the one hundred year experience of women police in Australia.

I have kept the account fairly succinct to keep it moving and keep the reader's interest. In some cases I have not been able to piece together the full sequence of events that led to a major change in a specific jurisdiction. Perhaps this is for the best — in providing something for a future project or for other scholars interested in the details of social change processes in major public sector institutions.

The experience of having grant applications rejected made me realise how disinterested or even hostile many academics are to the topic of women in policing and to a simple narrative account of discrimination and positive change. The idea that police are oppressive agents of social control tends to be common in universities, and has apparently closed the minds of many academics to the many benefits of professional policing and of women in policing. Over the years, in dealings with senior police, and many politicians and ministers, male and female, I have also been constantly amazed at the lack of interest in gender issues in policing. Time and again I have been utterly confused by the absence of any evidence of a sisterhood. Women police have been a beleaguered minority for many decades, but not just as a result of male ostracism. In many cases, senior women in government have done nothing to help.

On top of that, policing is, of course, a tough job, dealing with criminals and the constant threat of physical attack. Any woman who puts her hand up for the job of protecting the community as a police officer, and manages to carry out her duties in a competent and conscientious manner, in the teeth of a myriad of external and internal challenges, is to be greatly admired.

Tim Prenzler

About the Author

Tim Prenzler is Professor of Criminology and Program Coordinator of the Bachelor of Criminology and Justice at the University of the Sunshine Coast. From 2008 to 2014 he was a Chief Investigator in the Australian Research Council Centre of Excellence in Policing and Security, based at Griffith University, where he managed the Integrity Systems Project and worked in the Frontline Policing Project. He was also a foundation member of the School of Criminology and Criminal Justice at Griffith, from 1991. His research interests include gender in policing, crime prevention, corruption prevention, and police and security officer safety.

Acknowledgment

Thanks to the Queensland Police and New South Wales Police for photos printed in this book.

A Note on Referencing

Clippings from Queensland newspapers are a major source in this book. These clippings are contained in the 'Commissioners' Correspondence' file in the State Archives or were supplied to me by the Queensland Police Service. The clippings include the name of the newspaper and the date, but not the page number. In addition, quotations are included from current and former male and female police officers I interviewed for the Masters thesis. The thesis is referenced in the book, and the informants are referenced by number. Finally, it should be noted that the bulk of the memos, letters and reports from Queensland cited in the book are held in the State Archives.

Australia's first policewoman, Lilian Armfield, with NSW Police traffic branch officers Amy Millgate and Gladys Johnson, 1948.

Uniformed and plain clothes NSW policewomen, Superintendent's Office, Sydney 1955.

Chapter 1

Breaking In

This chapter analyses the processes that led to the establishment of the first policewomen in Australia. The first appointments were made in 1915, initially in New South and then South Australia. Most of the other states followed soon after. However, it was not until 1961 that all jurisdictions had female officers. The main initial factors behind this change were the social dislocations associated with World War One. There was a labour shortage in policing, enlarged concerns about the safety of women and girls, and concerns about the alleged negative effects of women on soldiers. The main political force was a loose coalition of women's groups, called the 'women police movement'. Male decision makers eventually buckled to the pressure and created a small space for female officers.

Background

In 1901, when Australia became a nation, there were no women police, and this appears to have been the situation around the world. The main driver of change was the women police movement, which developed in the early twentieth century in most Western countries in association with the women's suffrage movement advocating the right to vote and other social and political rights for women.[1] Women's charitable and political groups lobbied for a specialist group within the police to deal more effectively with women and girls caught between welfare institutions and the criminal justice system. Stuttgart, in Germany, has been attributed with the appointment of the first officially titled 'police woman' in 1903.[2] In the United States, the first policewoman proper is usually said to have been appointed in Los Angeles in 1910.

Australian newspapers carried positive accounts of these innovations, as in this report from Adelaide *Chronicle* in 1913 under the heading 'America's First Policewoman'[3]

> Mrs. Alice Stebbins Wells, whose portrait appears in our illustrated supplement this issue is the first policewoman in the United States and is attached to the Police Department of Los Angeles, California. She usually

works in plain clothes. Women police have also made their appearance for the first time in history in the streets of Philadelphia. They wear a blue uniform, and, like other members of the force, are provided with hand-cuffs and revolvers. Their special duty is to look after unprotected girls and to arrest obnoxious or disorderly persons who annoy them. Public opinion favors a larger number of policewomen, whose work, it is thought, will tend to improve the morals of the city.

In the same year, the Adelaide *Register* provided a similarly positive account:[4]

The experiment of women police appears to have been successful. Vancouver authorities have appointed female-constables, and there have been similar appointments in Seattle, San Francisco, and elsewhere. In 'Frisco there were more than 300 applications for three vacancies. The civic authorities are generally satisfied that women's work 'on beat' has proved highly salutary.

The women police movement received added impetus from the changed security situation and labour shortages produced by World War One. There were increases in female homelessness and lost or begging children. Women and children were vulnerable to the depredations of servicemen in training camps or in transit. Fears about the spread of sexually transmitted diseases amongst the armed forces led to concerted efforts to prevent potentially infectious contacts.[5] In London in 1914, women formed police volunteer organisations and were attested into the London Metropolitan Police in 1923.[6] During the war, women officers were engaged in part to police public and semi-public places that offered opportunities for dangerous liaisons. The London volunteer force provided a key reference point for the women police movement in Australia. In Western Australia, for example, women's groups who lobbied the Colonial Secretary cited the example of recent appointments in New South Wales and South Australia. They were, however,[7]

more mindful of the quasi-police role of the Voluntary Women Patrols set up in England by the National Union of Women Workers in late 1914. They did preventative work among women and girls near military camps, in munitions factories, and in parks.

Female police officers were appointed during the War or at the end of the war in the British Isles in Dublin, Grantham, Hull, Bristol and Birmingham; and in a number of locations in Canada, Austria, Germany and the United States.[8]

In Australia, the case for women police was promoted by women's charitable and political groups similar to those operating overseas. In 1911 the National Council of Women of Queensland (NCWQ) asserted that the police force needed 'trained social workers ... given the status of public officers ... to deal with girls in difficulty or danger, and to patrol parks and beaches'.[9] The National Council of Women (NCW) was established in 1902 with aims of general social improvement focused on disadvantaged women and children. The Council included 35 organisations, such as the Women's Christian Temperance Union, the Methodist Neglected Children's Aid Society and the Victorian Infant Asylum and Foundling Hospital.[10] 'Their collective muscle flexing was a force to be reckoned with'.[11] In one of its early successes, the Council pressured the Victorian Chief Secretary to employ female wardens and searchers in police cells.[12]

Table 1.1 shows the dates of establishment or consolidation of Australia's main police forces, and the dates when women were first appointed. The following sections of the chapter provide a narrative account of events leading up to the initial appointments in each jurisdiction:

Table 1.1 Timeline of Establishment of Australian Police Forces and Appointment of the First Female Officers

Jurisdiction	Police Force Establishment/ Consolidation	Appointment of Female Officers	Political Party in Power
New South Wales	1862	1915, July	Labor
South Australia	1838	1915, December	Labor
Victoria	1853	1917, July	Liberal
Western Australia	1853	1917, September	Nationalist
Tasmania	1899	1917, October	Liberal
Queensland	1864	1931	Country
Commonwealth	1917	1947	Labor
Northern Territory	1870	1961	Not applicable*

Note: * In 1961 the Northern Territory was governed by a federally appointed Administrator who consulted with a partially elected Legislative Council.

New South Wales

Vince Kelly, in his biography of Australia's first policewoman Lillian Armfield, describes the decision to appoint female officers in New South Wales as 'a move made grudgingly':[13]

It had been strongly pressed by influential women's organisations, and had been resisted by one Government after another, until in 1915 the politicians gave in. The women's organisations argued that women were more competent than men to deal with certain phases of crime, and with delinquent girls. They insisted that there should be women police to investigate offences perpetrated against women and children. They asserted that women police would bring to law enforcement a healthy reformative influence which would go a long way towards reclaiming women and girls from tendencies to immorality or crime.

According to Kelly, the turning point in the campaign occurred when the head of the police force Inspector-General James Mitchell 'threw his own weight behind it'. [14] Mitchell was aware of developments in regard to women police overseas and moves in that direction in South Australia.[15] He was also apparently exercised by the 'unsettling' effect of the war on young women, manifested in part by reports of hundreds of early-teen girls running away from home. Sydney was a major staging post for the war effort and the focus of many of these problems. The situation has been described as follows:[16]

> The advent of WWI resulted not only in a general slackening of community standards in metropolitan areas but, also an influx of young women. War, among other things, means concentrations of young men in uniform. Such men, on leave or in transit, were to be found in Sydney in large numbers. It was (and still is) the case that young women are greatly attracted to men in uniform. During 1914 and 1915 a considerable number of young women left their suburban and country homes in search of these young men and the glamour and good times associated with them. In seeking that good time many were simultaneously escaping restrictions and boring lives at homes. Often without thought for the future and with only a few coins in their purses young women newly arrived in the metropolis were easy prey for those who would exploit them. By 1915, the female influx had achieved problem proportions.

Another pressing factor was the enlistment of police in the military. The rush to join the fray had left the New South Wales Force 'seriously undermanned'.[17] Over 150 officers had left to join the military before police enlistments were banned in 1915.[18] According to Kelly:[19]

> With this picture in mind Mitchell decided that women police should be appointed. He was warned by the State Colonial Secretary, George Black, that Cabinet would only agree to their recruitment as an experiment, and that no extra money would be granted for the services of the policewomen. Their number would be restricted to two, and Mitchell could make his choice. If he wanted the policewomen, then he would have to do

without two male police. Mitchell was secretly amused. He realised that it would be impossible to keep up the strength of the police force in wartime to its approved quota, and this difficulty offered the opportunity to test the arguments for the value of policewomen. It was an experiment that was closely watched by women's organisations, and not less vigilantly by the male members of the force.

Swanton notes an additional factor that may have influenced Mitchell:

> Departmental folklore has it that Inspector-General Mitchell was influenced in part by the sight one day of male police arresting, not without a great deal of difficulty, a number of resisting females. Considering it an unedifying sight, he formed the view that it was preferable for females to arrest females.[20]

As indicated, support for women police had been expressed prior to the War. New South Wales' newspapers carried numerous enthusiastic accounts of the work of women police overseas, particularly in the United States, Canada and London. A typical example, from the Wagga Wagga *Daily Advertiser*, was published in March 1914, a few months before war broke out, under the heading 'Women as Police',[21]

> Chicago is greatly satisfied with its experiment with the police women, ten of whom were appointed last August to assist in the reforming of morals and manners of the great lake city. The experiment has proved to be so successful that Major Funkhouser, the Superintendent of Police, has asked the City Council to allow him to employ 15 more women police
>
> "The women blue coats," declared the major, "have done a wonderful amount of good. The ten we have had in the force have been assigned to dance-halls, and the curbing they have done there has been conducive to much good."
>
> The Council has agreed to the major's request and Chicago will have 25 women constables, all of whom (says a "Daily Chronicle" telegram) will be not only fearless, but strong and muscular officers who can hold their own, even when arresting men. In cases of actual arrest, however, the male officers are usually called upon, though the women police have taken men to the lock-up.

The *Sunday Times* carried a more detailed report in April 1914:[22]

POLICE WOMAN
WILL SHE ARRIVE IN SYDNEY?
WHAT SHE DOES IN OTHER PARTS OF THE WORLD

According to Inspector-General Day, the head of the N.S.
Wales police, there is no immediate chance of Sydney
seeing the 'police-woman ' on the streets in uniform, as
threatened in South Australia, and as is actually the case

in other parts of the world.

The idea of the police-woman is that the female officers could better deal with members of the weaker sex who go wrong, or who are in peril, than can ordinary policemen. The policeman and police-woman would patrol the parks, say, at night, together, and if a couple were seen behaving in such a manner as to arouse suspicion, the male officer would take charge of the man and the female constables would deal with the woman, either taking her to the watch-house if the circumstances of the case warranted, or give her a warning and some good advice.

At the police station, the duty of women officers would be to take the story of any female, or juvenile victims to assault, a sympathetic woman interrogator being more likely to elicit the true details than a man. The police-woman would be invested with powers to PROTECT YOUNG GIRLS seen in doubtful company, and to generally act as guide, philosopher, and friend.

It will be seen that much would depend upon the sort of women employed in this work, and that they would have to be possessed of very special personal qualities.

In Glasgow for some time now a corps of women have been employed by a Vigilance Committee, working with the help and sympathy of the general police. It is now proposed to create an official staff of police-women as such.

The police-woman already exists in Germany, in Canada, and in parts of the United States. These female officers have been working now for a number of years, and testimony from all quarters is that the results are of a most satisfactory character.

Asked by a 'Sunday Times' representative if the Police Department of N.S. Wales had ever contemplated taking, similar steps, Mr. Day said that the formation of a corps of women police had certainly not been considered. Personally, he did not, at first glance, regard it as desirable. 'You would want a special corps of male police to look after them,' he said.

THE POSITION IN SYDNEY.

'If we had police-women,' he continued, 'we would use

them in such a way that the public would not recognise them. They would not wear uniforms, and we would arrange that their evidence would not be given in the courts. We already employ women at times to assist us, and they work under those conditions. Whenever the circumstances arose we could easily employ more. Certainly women officers, if they were the right ones, could do special work more effectually than men. They might be able to work among young girls or children.

'If there was ANY 'WHITE SLAVE' TRAFFICER we would probably use women freely, keeping them, as I have indicated.

But there is no evidence that anything of the sort is going on. The woman assistant is right, but I cannot say that the time has come here for the appointment of the woman police constable. There is not the same sort of work to do here that there is in Glasgow or some of the cities of America.'

___

Newspapers in New South Wales also began to carry reports about the possible introduction of women police in Victoria, and lobbying there by the National Council of Women.[23] Again, reporting was generally positive, sometimes enthusiastic, but with some exceptions. 'How about women as police?' asked *The Sydney Stock and Station Journal:*[24]

> There is no role in which she is not ambitious enough to play a part. The female member of the species has designs on almost every job occupied by the brute half of the race—even that of being a man. They think that they have a mission now to reform the 'roughs' of Melbourne, and want to join the 'force.' Strangely enough, the idea is apt to commend itself to Mr. J. Murray, the Chief Secretary, and before long the visiting Sydneyite will see the spectacle of a lot of hard-faced, hardhearted hussies patrolling the streets of the Southern capital. It would be funny if it were not so pathetic. The weaker-sex snap up every opportunity of quitting the sacred-side of the home. Independence is their cry — irresponsible independence. The ambition is no doubt laudable, but is it desirable?

In April and May of 1915, stories began to appear about the inclusion of women police in plans by the New South Wales Colonial Secretary George Black to reorganise the police department. Black was Colonial Secretary in the Labor government from 15 March 1915 to 15 November 1916.[25] The *Albury Banner and Wodonga Express* reported that 'The matter was under consideration before he came into office, but nothing was decided'. The paper went on:[26]

> If any appointments are made, they will be only for the metropolitan area, and the women police will deal solely with members of their own sex. "I am: only considering the matter in a general way," remarked Mr. Black. "It is one of the subjects which is going to be considered when I go into the reorganisation of the police force with the Inspector-General. If we did anything, only a few women would be required, but the difficulty would be to get the right sort— women with considerable force of character, and strength of body. Not viragos, but strong, reputable women of very high character. I see a difficulty in getting the women, should we want them". Mr Black pointed out that a considerable amount of good was already being done by the Salvation Army and other aid societies, who rendered valuable assistance to female immigrants, who were friendless and unprotected in a strange country.

A week later, newspapers reported that a deputation from the Citizens' Association had met the 'Chief Secretary' about lack of facilities and activities for working young people and their consequent exposure to vice.[27] The group also advocated the appointment of women police, and Black reportedly said he would take the issue to the Premier and Cabinet. On Wednesday 2 June, newspapers reported that the government had decided upon an 'experiment' with two women officers, and included a recruitment notice. As one example, *The Leader*, based in Orange, reported as follows:[28]

> The Chief Secretary, Mr Black, stated this afternoon that it had been decided to appoint two police women as an experiment, their services to be mainly devoted to the protection of girls and women. Should this experiment prove a success the number of police women will be increased.
>
> Applicants should be under 30 years of age, and capable of enduring hardship and fatigue, of good character and address and fair average education.

On Saturday June 5, *The Sydney Morning Herald* reported on a visit from Women's Progressive Association to the Chief Secretary to congratulate him on the decision and 'urge other reforms':[29]

POLICE WOMEN.
THE NEW DEPARTURE.
PROTECTION OF GIRLS.

A few days ago there appeared in the newspapers an advertisement signed by the Inspector-General of Police, pointing out that applications were invited for women police ...

Yesterday afternoon a deputation from the Women's Progressive Association waited on the Chief Secretary (Mr. Black) to congratulate him on making this departure, and to urge other reforms.

Miss A. Golding, president of the association, said that the step the Minister had taken was a proper one, and ought to have been made long before.

The Minister had not been here a week before he put the matter in hand.

Miss Golding remarked that she had noticed that it was intended only to appoint two or three women police for the present. She hoped the Minister would increase the number. Women police were badly needed at such places as the Central Railway Station, through which so many thousands of boys and girls passed daily on their way to and from school. There were precocious naughty boys and girls, and boys who had to be saved from themselves. There should be more supervision in the parks. She considered that the wearing of uniforms would militate against the usefulness of the women police.

Black fielded a number of other suggestions from the group regarding social improvements. The paper also reported that the women would wear uniforms and have full police powers.

After the two positions were advertised in late-May, newspapers reported there were more than 400 applications.[30] This was despite the fact that:

> The pay was only seven and sixpence per day. There was no guarantee of continuity of employment, no uniform, no overtime payments, no expenses of any sort, not even for the fares paid by the women in connection with their duty.[31]

The two appointees began work on 1 July 1915. Lillian Armfield's previous work as a mental health nurse at Callan Park Mental Hospital, and her strong build and natural intelligence, appeared to fit her perfectly for the new role. Maude Rhodes had been an Inspector in Sydney with the Children's Relief Department and had experience working with police.

Although the new officers reportedly had sat the same entrance exam as the men, once appointed they side stepped the standard 12 week pre-service training course. In addition, unlike male officers, who were fully sworn after training and began in uniform with a subsequent competitive process for selection to plain clothes detective duties, the women began work in plainclothes and were sworn in as Special Constables on a probationary basis for 12 months. Swanton reports that this downgrading of the women's status was the result of the need to circumvent rules about age in the case of Armfield. Again, 'according to departmental legend',[32]

> Miss Armfield understated her age in her job application. Born on 3rd December, 1884, she was eighteen months over the age limit. No deceit was apparently intended, as evidence by the department's determination to employ her. However, the Police Regulation Act 1899 precluded the hiring of regular police employees over 30 years of age. It was thus decided, so the story goes, to employ the two women as Special Constables as no age limit applied with respect to such appointments. Forty-nine years were to pass before this massive disadvantage in conditions of female service was finally rectified in 1965.

The precarious and secondary status of the new officers was also marked by a requirement that they sign an indemnity releasing the police force from any legal liabilities for their safety and agreeing not to make any claims on the police pension fund.[33]

South Australia

The appointments in New South Wales were followed five months later by two in South Australia on 1 December 2015. As noted, South Australian newspapers had reported favourably on women police overseas. In 1913, in an interview with Vida Goldstein, President of the Victorian Women's Political Association, who was visiting Adelaide, *The Register* asked if there was 'any special object you are aiming at in Adelaide?' Goldstein — described as 'dark, pretty, and vivacious' and making 'a charming conversation'— replied as follows:[34]

> The appointment of women matrons in the lockups. It is astonishing that men should attend to women in the lockups. We have got that reform in Victoria, although it took 15 years to obtain. Then we want to have women police to attend to women and children and young people generally. They should have power to arrest, but their work would be more in the direction of helping those whom they see are treading dangerous paths. There is a great need for these officials at picture theatres and other

places. We believe that women should be appointed to offices in which they are naturally more capable than men. There is to be an inspector under the Maternity Act. That should be a woman. But, no, the Government closed the door to all but men.

Subsequently, *The Mail* reported that it had spoken to the President of the Women's Non-Party Political Association, Mrs. J.P. Morice, who reported that the Association had made a deputation to the Chief Secretary advocating, among other things, for the appointment of women matrons to the police watchhouse.[35]

The broad social conditions in Adelaide were similar to those in Sydney, although the situation in relation to young women and soldiers was less pronounced and the decision-making process was more conflicted. One of the appointees, Kate Cocks, and another woman had already been engaged in patrol work in parks and streets as employees of the State Children's Department.[36] Their work in rescuing girls from dangerous liaisons, including escorting them home and talking to their parents, relied on voluntary compliance. Although no issues of non-compliance were reported, the potential for difficulties was recognised. In February 1914, the Secretary of the State Children's Council, Mr J. Gray, wrote to the Chief Secretary, the Honourable J.G. Brice, noting 'the advisability of appointing a small number of police women who duties shall be for the protection of the morals of young girls'.[37] The Officer-in-Charge of the Police Metropolitan Division, an Inspector Burchell, advised the Chief Secretary that the appointment of more male officers was a more pressing priority. He also observed that that it would be too difficult to supervise and protect women police involved in combatting 'social evil' at night.[38] He conceded a potential role for female officers with police powers in the State Children's Department. But they would be 'quite useless to the police'.[39] The Police Commissioner, W. H. Raymond, supported his Inspector's views, recommending to the Chief Secretary that patrolling duties would be better carried out by women from philanthropic organisations.[40]

In its annual report for 2014, the State Children's Council maintained its position.[41] In March 1914, *The Register*, 'apropos of the progressive spirit of the times' regarding the employment of women, advocated the appointment of women police to patrol Adelaide's 'parks, streets, and places of entertainment to protect and advise the young and unwary girls, who seem to have unrestricted liberty and licence.'[42] The newspaper also claimed 'there is urgent need for women's work in conjunction with the Children's Courts and State Children's Department' and applauded the Women's Non-Party Political Association, who it reported 'have made repeated appeals to the Chief Secretary (Hon. J. G. Brice) to appoint a police matron'. One area of work that was singled out was escorting neglected children.

In February 1915, *The Register* reported favourably on developments with women police in the United States and Britain.[43] The issue received further exposure in the media when a member of the Women's Non-Party Political Association, Margaret Wragge, spoke at a meeting in April 1915. Ms Wragge argued that police had a poor image and standards needed to be improved:[44]

> The raising process is most necessary for what body of public servants is more ridiculed for their inefficiency, for their obsolete methods, for their clumsy tactics, than the present day police?

This dim view of the male constabulary echoed an earlier letter to the editor, from 'a widow', published in *The Advertiser* in 1914:[45]

> The Rev. L. B. Fletcher is quite right in what he says about Port Adelaide … There is too much gambling, drinking, and sly-grog selling. There is a sly-grog shop not far from where I live. Men are going there all day Sunday. When I spoke to the police about it they said they have to catch the offenders. They can do nothing because this place keeps boarders. Why are people allowed to have a cellar full of drink because they keep boarders? That is only an excuse. A few women police would soon catch these men.

In February 1914, *The Mail* referred to suggestions for women police in Adelaide and 'success' with the idea overseas, going on to publish the following satire:[46]

Some folk are never satisfied,

If what we hear is true.

They're not content with men alone,

They want a Girl in Blue.

A new idea they've conjured up

The wave of sin to stop;

And so they talk of swearing in

A constable Jane Hop.

We see her garbed in uniform,

A figure trim and neat;

Replica, of a bobby bold,

But minus bobby's feet.

She swings a baton in her hand,

And not a broom or mop;

And fellows with a passing wink

Salute the new Jane Hop...

At night where will her duty lie?

We long to know the street

Where Jane with baton, cuffs, and all,

Will pace upon her beat.

Some ardent swain will seek her out.

And as she is a cop,

She will arrest his heart, and then

No more we'll know Jane Hop.

The Social Reform Bureau, representing 16 charity and religious groups, was able to obtain a meeting with the new Chief Secretary, A.W. Styles, on 27 April 1915. *The Register* reported that the deputation emphasised the success of women police in numerous locations overseas, collegial relations between male and female officers, and male gratitude for being excused from 'irksome but necessary duties' in relation to women.[47] One of the speakers was Miss B.E. Dixon from the Travellers' Aid Society. She had been engaged in rescuing young women from procurement for prostitution at transport hubs, but she argued that a female police officer would carry greater authority in dealing with the problem. Chief Secretary Styles promised the deputation that Cabinet would discuss the matter in the near future. A New South Wales newspaper reported that Styles told the deputation 'he was satisfied an alteration of the present methods was necessary. With regard to the form that alteration should take, he was not prepared to speak'.[48]

Further pressure was applied after the State Children's Council, responding to a proposal from St Mary's Mission of Hope, set up a sub-committee to review the issue. St Mary's Mission offered to provide two female patrol officers to work under the supervision of Kate Cocks patrolling public areas between 7.30 and 11.30 p.m. The Council supported the proposal in principle but wanted the women located within the police department, with full powers. The sub-committee's report was forwarded to Styles in June. In early-July the Governor announced the government's plans to create female patrols. The Police Commissioner attempted to persuade the Chief Secretary of the virtue of locating the female patrol officers as adjuncts of the State Children's Department.[49] His recommendation included a report by Edward Priest, Sub-Inspector of Detectives, advocating the creation of a new Act to employ women as 'State Guards, lady State Officers or State Protection Officers', with the claim that women 'police' would be treated with suspicion as spies.[50] However, by this time, the government appeared convinced of the case for women police and the way was cleared with legal advice from Crown Solicitor that the Police Act allowed for the swearing in of women as constables.[51]

Advertisements were placed in daily newspapers in Adelaide on 27 September. On 7 November the Chief Secretary announced in the Legislative Assembly that women patrols would begin duty on 1 December. The new officers 'will be treated the same as constables in regard to hours of labour and remuneration'.[52] There were over 20 applications 'from women from all walks of life. Many were nurses, church workers and teachers, and the remainder domestics, barmaids, dressmakers, postmistresses and stenographers'.[53] Kate Cocks did not submit an application, apparently telling Margaret Wragge that she 'she did not believe in seeking appointments but that if the position were offered she would accept it'.[54] She was in fact informed by the Police Commissioner, two days before applications closed, that she would be appointed as the Officer-in-Charge of the Women Police, beginning 1 December.[55] Styles reportedly offered Cocks six assistants. However, given the many uncertainties of the new program, she opted for just one additional member and selected Annie Ross, who was an Assistant Inspectress of lying-in homes.[56] The South Australian appointments were reportedly the first involving equal standing for female officers with their male colleagues in British Empire countries.[57]

Victoria

In Victoria, in the years before the War, the National Council of Women was concerned about an alleged 'white slave trade' involving the kidnapping of young women for enforced prostitution.[58] Denials by the authorities did little to reduce their concerns. In August 2014, a South Australian newspaper *The Advertiser* carried the following story:[59]

POLICE WOMEN. WILL THEY
BE APPOINTED IN VICTORIA?

Mr. J. Murray, the Chief Secretary, intends to consult Mr. A. G. Sainsbury, the Chief Commissioner of Police, as to the desirability of strengthening the police force by the appointment of women constables to do special work. The Minister is doubtful as to the practicability of the reform. "There may be a few things that a policewoman might be able to do better than a policeman," said Mr. Murray, "but I am quite sure that there are a great many duties that a policeman has to perform that a policewoman could not do, and that it would not be fair or expedient to ask her to do. However, the experiment of having women police has been tried elsewhere. We have no detailed statements as to the results of their work. Perhaps the Chief Commissioner of Police is better informed and can advise me. It is a wonder that police-women have not been appointed to assist in keeping the suffragettes in order. It is true that we have matrons on duty at the city lockup that attend to women arrested and charged with offences. They are doing good work as far as I know, but that is different work from what policewomen would be called upon to do if their duties were to be anything like those of policemen. Possibly policewomen could make certain enquiries in con- nection with criminal investigation better than some policemen. I can only promise enquiry."

In May of 1915, the National Council of Women discussed a proposal from the Society for the Prevention of Cruelty to Children for 'the appointment of women police for the greater protection of girls and children, and the collection of evidence in certain cases'.[60] The proposal included the idea of female magistrates and jurors for court cases involving women and children. A representative of the Sex Hygiene and Morality Council at the meeting advocated female officers wear uniforms and have the power of arrest. In June 1915, Chief Commissioner Sainsbury wrote to the NSW Inspector of Police seeking information on the system in NSW. Sainsbury noted that it was probably too early for firm evidence but was interested in any information, including employment conditions.[61] Any reply from New South Wales appears to have been lost.

Vida Goldstein and Adela Pankhurst from the Women's Political Association (WPA) were able to obtain a meeting with the Chief Secretary Murray. The meeting covered a range of issues but the appointment of women police was at the top of the list.[62] Pankhurst was the Organiser of the WPA and followed up on the meeting with a letter to Chief Commissioner Sainsbury asking that he meet with 'a deputation of ladies … to place before you the many reasons we have for wishing to see appointed a certain number of women police'.[63] The letter added that[64]

> We would like to inform you of what we saw in New South Wales of the women's work. In the opinion of the Chief Secretary, Mr Black, the work of the women has been so effective that he is appointing four more.

Sainsbury replied that the government had already considered the proposal and decided against it: 'It will be useless therefore for your Association to see me on the subject'.[65]

Sainsbury's response appears to have been a convenient misrepresentation of 'the Government's' position. On July 1, *The Argus* reported that Chief Secretary Murray was 'somewhat favourably disposed to the idea', so long as 'the right stamp of women' were employed.[66] Despite this 'small nod of approval', Murray 'knew senior police were scathingly critical'.[67] Murray had sought opinion from inside the force and the results were not good. An Inspector O'Sullivan thought that women's time would be better spent supervising their children. On the question of evidence gathering, he thought that 'police have at all times been able to collect evidence of any nature required in any cases.'[68] If women collected evidence, male police would have to go over it afterwards to have it be of any use or complete it'.[69] Part of the problem was that male police managers appeared to see the idea of women police as a personal criticism of their performance. Superintendent Gleeson could see absolutely no benefit from women police in terms of improved safety for women. He saw a particular danger in women's involvement in sexual crimes:[70]

> To have an unduly sympathetic or emotional policewoman investigating the carefully prepared but probably concocted statement of another woman alleging rape against a man, might, and I say so from experience, easily bring an innocent man within measurable distance of the gallows.

The Superintendent of the CIB, where women police would most likely be located, added that he could not see any value from women police and that the type of work envisaged should be carried out by charities. He added that, 'As to the preparing of evidence all I need to say on the subject is where are the women to be found that know what is evidence.'[71] An unsigned and unaddressed memo from the Chief Commissioner's office also indicated a personal animus against women. If women police were introduced 'as an experiment' they should be the relatives of soldiers who fought in the War, not 'self-advertising and self-seeking females who possibly have, in some degree, been actuated by self-interested motives'.[72]

As evidence emerged about the success of the women officers in New South Wales, *The Argus* reported on increasing support from Murray.[73] However, he was unwilling to take action and retired at the end of 1915. It took the new Chief Secretary Donald McLeod the better part of a year to decide in favour of the proposal. In August 1916, under the headline 'POLICEWOMEN Two to be appointed', *The Argus* reported that[74]

> The home secretary of the National Council of Women (Mrs D. Skene) received yesterday a communication from the Chief Secretary (Mr McLeod) announcing that the Government had decided to accede to the request of the National Council and appoint two police-women. Mr McLeod also said that the executive of the national council would be asked to recommend suitable candidates for the positions. The salaries of the new officials would be set at £90 per annum.

Several days later McLeod told parliament that the new appointments would be a 'trial', the appointees would not be sworn and that they would 'specialise' in welfare work with women.[75]

Ninety applications were reportedly received, but the hopes of all the applicants were quickly dashed. On 30 December, *The Argus* reported that the Chief Secretary had decided 'the need for economy was greater than the need for policewomen' and plans were moth-balled.[76] However, as Colleen Woolley reports in her history of women police in Victoria, a consensus of sorts, and set of strong expectations, had been built around the need for female police officers to protect women and girls. Seven months after the great anticlimax, tucked away on page 8 of July 30 edition of *The Argus*, was a very brief announcement that two policewoman would be sworn in that day.[77] In fact, Mrs Madge Connor and Miss Elizabeth Beers had been sworn in two days earlier, and 'the experiment had finally begun'.[78]

Tasmania

The background to the introduction of women police in Tasmania is somewhat shadowy. The Attorney General in the Liberal government was William Propsting. His wife was a member of the WCTU and NCWT, but no evidence of pillow talk on the issue of women police has come to light and there are no minute books available from the WCTU for that period. It appears though that the WCTU most likely approached the Attorney-General on the issue around March 1917.[79] The first appointment was made in October 1917. Available evidence suggests Police Commissioner Andrewartha was supportive.[80] *The Daily Post* reported that, 'It was the intention of the Attorney-General not to appoint policewomen til the money had been voted, but he changed his mind'[81] — implying that the Attorney-General was the instigator. In similar terms, *The Examiner* stated, 'It was decided by the Attorney-General to make a beginning by appointing two police-women, but so far only one has been selected'.[82]

According to the Tasmanian *Police Register*, the first female Police Constable was Kate Evelyn Campbell.[83] She was followed by Maud Lillian Cross and Maud Mersey Hughes. Campbell's previous employ-ment is not recorded. She joined the Force on 10 October 1917 in Hobart, and was 'discharged' for unrecorded reasons on January 8, 1918. Cross and Hughes had been engaged in domestic duties. Cross, from Hobart, listed as single, joined on 1 June 1918 at the age of 29. She was assigned to Launceston on 25 November 1918 and resigned on 31 August 1922. Hughes, listed as married, from Devonport, was 30 when she was appointed at Hobart on 6 February 1918. She resigned on 31 May 1921. Following Cross's departure, Launceston was without a female officer until 1940, and it was not until 1944 that Burnie received an appointee.[84]

There is considerable mystery regarding Kate Campbell's origins, experiences on the job, sudden discharge and subsequent fate. The Commissioners' Correspondence for the period is missing, and newspapers were silent regarding this loss to the new office they had supported. In 1979, a journalist interviewed one of Tasmania's earliest policewomen. According to Jean Priest, who was 81 at the time of the interview and had been appointed in 1921, 'One of her predecessors was caught riding a tram with a detective, and was dismissed after three months'.[85] This appears to be the only extant explanation regarding the brief tenure of Tasmania's first female police officer. Kate Campbell was married when appointed, as was Maude Hughes, but it is probable they were widowed and without children. Jean Priest recalled that married women were not allowed to join, although exceptions were made, as in her own case. She had to provide two medical certificates to prove her husband's war wounds were incurable and that he could not provide for her.[86]

Western Australia

Women's groups in Western Australia also took up the issue of women police from the break out of war, citing the example of women's patrols in England and, subsequently, the work of the new female officers in Sydney and Adelaide. The Women's Service Guild of Western Australia 'were most assertive petitioners directing their requests uncompromisingly to the Minister of Police, the Colonial Secretary and the Commissioner of Police'.[87] *The Sunday Times* in Perth reported in 1914, that 'The Women's Christian Temperance Union propose to have women policemen for duty in public parks and other recreation reserves'[88]. This was then followed by a comic poem attributed to 'Dryblower':

The vagrant who friskily flirts

　And gives every girl a glad eye,

Will be settled by something-in-skirts

　Who'll handy be hovering by.

Even so much as a wink

Will earn him a wrap from a rod,

While proposals peculiar and pink

Will get him a sixer in quod,

But 'twill solace them when they are gaoled,

And somewhat alleviate pain,

When the criminal knows he was nailed

By a pretty young John Hop named

Jane!

In 1916, several newspapers reported on the issue of women police. In early-February, *The Daily News* reported that in December of 1915 the Women's' Club had petitioned Mr. A. E. Green, M.L.A. on 'the need of women police for the protection of young girls'.[89] Green referred the issue to the Premier, who consulted with the Police Commissioner. An extract from the Commissioner's formal response to the Colonial Secretary was quoted in the newspaper:

> From a long experience and after consulting a number of the senior officers of the police, I am of opinion that the type of women required is a middle aged, experienced person of lovable nature (a trained nurse if possible), who by kindness can persuade these unfortunate girls that they are on the road to ruin. Indeed I am clearly of opinion that in performing her duties she should display as little of the police as possible if she is to be at all successful in her work. I think it would be a great mistake to enrol an untrained woman and vest her with all the powers of a constable without first giving her a thorough training. In my opinion the best course to adopt would be to appoint additional female inspectors and attach them to the State Children's Department, and if later on it was found that they proved themselves capable there would be no objection to appointing them special constables.[90]

The issue was reportedly being considered by the Cabinet.

The Western Australian Police Association published a hostile opinion piece in the July 1917 edition of its journal: 'To expect women to take up the duties of an ordinary policeman would be extremely absurd, yea impossible'.[91] It was treated as a self-evident fact that women could not deal with 'every offence and violation of the law whether it affects man or woman'.[92] What was left for women to do in police work once the tasks only men could perform were subtracted?

Nothing it appeared. The work of so-called female police in England and Cape Town was supposedly 'analysed' to illustrate the point:[93]

> In England, among other duties, the women police search female ammunition workers prior to their entering the factories, examine passports, attend to complaints from parents concerning misconduct of boys and girls, keeping an eye on wives in the absence of their husbands, illegitimate baby cases, cautioning wayward girls, etc., all these duties, although of a commendable character, are not the work of the police, and rightly so.

The anonymous author went on to support a role for women in addressing social problems but as volunteer social workers not police officers. In conclusion, the safety of women was raised as a final obstacle:

> It would be extremely dangerous for [women police] to frequent the haunts of immoral women alone. The class of female who require the supervision of the arm of the law are usually found in the slum portions of our cities, where congregate the most immoral of both sexes, and to expect a woman policeman to control this class under such circumstances would be absurd. Unfortunately, there is work to be done in our cities, especially among young girls and women, that can only be touched on by their own sex, but it is a problem we believe, that can only find a solution among the societies of women and religious bodies.[94]

Despite such negative views, Cabinet decided in favour of two positions some time in 1917.[95] Unfortunately, the records around the final decision making process appear to be lost, although it seems that the Colonial Secretary Harry Colebatch prevailed against Commissioner Robert Connell.[96] Once the decision was made, the appointment process was fairly swift. *The Sunday Times* printed prominent photos of the 'the two policewomen who have been appointed in the city' above the following report on the 9 September 1917:[97]

> They commenced duty last Monday. Mrs (Helen) Dugdale is a trained nurse and inspector, and previous to her appointment as a female-constable was connected with the Charities and State Children's Department. Miss (Laura) Chipper has been engaged for the past 15 years in the social work of the Salvation Army. As the lady-cops do not wear any distinctive uniform there's a very lively time in store for the pasty-faced young woman of the white-top boots and the expensive furs.

In the November issue of its journal, the Police Association included a very positive Letter-to-the-Editor from 'Wombat', who claimed 'women police are very heartily welcomed by the Force', arguing that many officers recognised that women could be better at some tasks.[98] More generally, according to Wombat[99]

> The idea of women police is not a new one, only confined to W.A., but it is of world-wide character. There are some people who imagine that a policeman's chief job is running in drunks. Those people do not know of the work the police are called upon to perform, and naturally their idea of women police was that of an Amazon capable of handling burly offenders.

The December edition of the Association's journal provided a surprisingly neutral account of the appointments. Although the new officers were reportedly sworn in under the Police Act, their work was described as not involving normal police duties, but closely associated allied with those of State Children Department inspectors. Eleven duties were cited: [100]

> (1) To keep young children from the streets, more especially at night; (2) to assist, where necessary, the Education Department in the prevention of truancy from school; (3) to watch the newspapers and furnish reports of persons endeavouring to decoy young girls by advertisements or any other means; (4) to patrol stations and visit picture shows, theatres, and other places of public entertainment, in order to guard and advise women, girls, and children who are strangers and have no friends waiting for them; (5) to patrol slum neighbourhoods, and look after drunken women, and to obtain assistance for their neglected children; (6) to keep under observation reputed brothels, wine shops, hotels, and other places frequented by women of ill fame, in order to prevent young girls being decoyed and drugged with liquor and entrapped; (7) to protect women and girls in the public parks and gardens , and when going to and leaving work; (8) to make inquiries for the State Children department and Charities Department in cases where it is desirable that the inquiry should be made by the police ion plainclothes; (9) to watch over and safeguard unprotected and innocent girls against unscrupulous employers and other persons; (10)to keep a separate file for all young women and girls whom they endeavour by their assistance to put on the straight path, such file to record their movements and behaviour until the officer is satisfied that they have either reformed or become incorrigible; (11) duties to be performed in plain clothes, and the hours of duties will be eight hours a day or more as required, at times best suited to their carrying out, and such duties to be arranged by the inspector in charge.

Queensland

As noted above, in Queensland the NCWQ advocated for women police as far back as 1911.[101] Newspapers took up the issue in 1915, the second year of the war, prompting the Acting Home Secretary

John Huxham to write to Police Commissioner William Cahill, requesting his opinion. Cahill stated, 'I am quite unable to indicate how women could be advantageously employed... In any event, I can assure you that we have old women in sufficient numbers in the Police Force already'.[102] Huxham was known as a supporter of women's suffrage and of the right for women to stand for parliament.[103] However, the *Telegraph* reported that he was 'not enamoured of the idea' of women police, and proposed to await the results of 'experiments in this direction in the southern states'.[104] Consequently, the war years passed without change.

Lobbying of the Commissioner and the government escalated in the late-1920s. The powerful Catholic Archbishop of Queensland, Duhig, came out in support, as did the Country Women's Association, the Australian Federation of Women Voters, the Queensland Women's Electoral League, along with the NCWQ.[105] Comparisons were made repeatedly with Britain, the United States and the other Australian states. South Australia was held up as a model[106]. Advocates employed a variety of arguments to try to persuade the government of the merit of appointing women police. The *Brisbane Daily Mail* argued that males lacked the sensitivity to deal with crime problems faced by women and girls.[107] The advantage to the police in preventing suspicions of improper dealings with girls under interrogation was emphasised, alongside the right of women to be dealt with by women. The conventional idea of the innate nurturing qualities of women was evoked as a vital element in potential reform.[108] The campaign was provided with further fuel by a 1928 report on the white slave trade, made to the League of Nations, which recommended that women police should be appointed in all countries[109]. The police and the government remained unmoved. 'Prejudice dies hard', declared the *Brisbane Courier*, 'and it appears to be dying very hard in Queensland in the matter of women police'.[110]

In 1929, the NCWQ made a further approach to the Home Secretary, who directed the Commissioner to investigate developments in other jurisdictions. Commissioner Ryan reported favourably on the work of women in the southern states and reported on a resolution in favour of the appointment of women — 'in their proper sphere' — passed by the 1927 Conference of the Police Commissioners of Australia. Ryan told the Home Secretary that 'I incline to the belief that such an appointment would meet the wishes of a great number of people of this State, who have approached me on the matter'. He suggested that the appointment of two women could be given a trial.[111]

Despite Ryan's apparent enthusiasm, he was not sufficiently interested to initiate action. The turning point came with the election of the first female member of state parliament. Irene Longman won the seat of Bulimba, in Brisbane, when Labor lost power to the Country Party in the Depression year of 1929. She subsequently lost her seat when Labor was returned to government in 1932. Mrs Longman had a strong interest in child welfare, especially as it related to the criminal justice system. She had been President of the NCWQ from 1921 to 1925 and held office in several reform societies.[112] In August 1930 Mrs Longman made a submission to Cabinet outlining the advantages of employing policewomen and at the end of 1930 a decision was made in favour of the proposal. The final element in the process may have been a visit by the Home Secretary, J.C. Petersen, to New South Wales. The New South Wales Police Commissioner spoke highly of the work done by women police and Petersen was impressed by the wide range of their welfare related duties.[113]

The decision was met with vehement opposition by the police union.[114] The change came at a time of dissension over relative reductions in staff and wages and increased duties.[115] The prospective appointment of women had been repeatedly described as an experiment and the union argued that there had been 'far too many costly experiments adopted by this state, and, unfortunately, many of them are now proving colossal failures, as the appointment of women police undoubtedly will be'.[116] The Union could see no role for women other than as 'ornaments' and stated bitterly that the appointments would only make the job harder than it already was. The only hope for the beleaguered males was that 'these lady police will do what naturalists say is done by a certain species of South American spider'.[117]

Irene Longman's single term in parliament gave leverage to the action taken by women's groups over several decades. Zara Dare and Eileen O'Donnell were selected from amongst 38 listed candidates and were appointed as policewomen on 16 March 1931. Dare (aged 44) had been an organiser in the Women's Christian Temperance Union (WCTU) and served with the Salvation Army in China where her work included rescuing women from prostitution.[118] O'Donnell worked keeping house for her brother. She heard of moves to introduce policewomen and wrote a letter of application with references from two state parliamentarians. She was 34 when appointed. Both women were single.

Commonwealth

Australia's Commonwealth Police Force was established in 1917. Despite the fact that women police were in place in other jurisdictions at the time, the appointment of women police at the national level did not appear to be an issue. The history of federal policing is marked by recurring structural change and various split responsibilities in guarding, policing and border protection. New South Wales Police were responsible for regular policing of the Australian Capital Territory (ACT) up until 1927, when the Australian Capital Territory Police was established (also known as the Federal Capital Territory Police).[119] Mrs Cook, the wife of the ACT's first police officer, Sergeant Phillip J. Cook, is attributed with performing the first female police duties in the ACT on a voluntary basis. She reportedly assisted her husband and 'assumed his role during his absences'.[120] In one incident,[121]

> The story goes that two girls had robbed their father and a boarder and hired a car for £20 to escape to Sydney. Mrs Cook called every police station along the Queanbeyan to Sydney route, giving notice of the offence. As a result, the girls were caught at Liverpool.

In her brief history of women in federal policing, Barbara M. Osborn notes that the utilisation of police officers' wives was a recurring practice. This evidenced the need for female officers, 'but formal requests submitted to superiors, were rejected, sometimes for rather ridiculous reasons by today's standards'.[122] In June 1942, Chief Officer H.E. Jones reported to the Secretary of the Attorney-General's Department that an Advisory Council recommended creating two positions for female officers.[123] He added that in his views the positions were currently unnecessary. In January 1943, an Acting Inspector, G.L. Smith, recommended the appointment of a 'Police Matron' for '(a) searching female prisoners; (b) escorting females; and (c) assisting regular members of the service in such work as requires the presence of a woman'.[124]

In February 1944, in a memo to the Attorney-General's Department Secretary concerning restructuring of the ACT Police, Chief Officer R. Reid including a paragraph supporting a female appointment:[125]

> This is a matter requiring early consideration, and I certainly recommend a police woman to deal with females and be in a position to move freely amongst the female population, especially females in custody and juvenile delinquents.

Despite this, nothing happened until 1947, when Alice Clarke was appointed as a sworn member of the force on July 18, with the addition of Mavis Chatfield on the July 28.[126]

Northern Territory

The Northern Territory was established as a self-governing entity in 1978. Up to that time, for most of the 20th Century, the area was under federal control. Despite the fact that women were appointed in the ACT in 1947, it was not until February1961 that the first women police were appointed in the far north. The idea dates back to at least 1957, involving discussions within the police and subsequently between the Territory Administrator and the Director of Welfare.[127] There was support from the District Welfare Officer in Darwin for assistance from female police officers for welfare officers 'in many matters associated with the welfare of older girls, young women and part-coloured women'.[128] Acting Superintendent of Police J.W. Stokes also wrote to the Police Commissioner in 1958, concluding that 'If it be conceded that we have a juvenile delinquent problem here and that women are better than men at solving it, it would seem desirable that we enlist Women Police to deal with it'.[129]

An additional factor playing into the decision to appoint women police was a staff shortage and the limited success of recruitment efforts in 1960.[130] The proposal for female officers was approved by the Commissioner and the Minister and the first female police in the Northern Territory began work on the 10th April 1961.[131] Five women were appointed: Margaret Craven, Shirley Booth, Fay Barton, Norma Bailey and Johanna Wendler. [132]The women went through the same recruit training course as the men prior to their appointment. Joyce Richardson from the South Australian Policewomen's Section was seconded to organise the new group in

June. It was reported that 'her pleasing personality and confident level headed approach to her work proved invaluable in establishing an efficient policewomen's section at Darwin'.[133]

Conclusion

This chapter provided a narrative account of the social and political processes leading to the introduction of women police officers in Australia. It is not an edifying story, especially for a new nation deemed to be vibrant democracy, a bastion of equality and a progressive social laboratory. A very small opening was created for women police as a result of repeated lobbying, mainly by women's groups. In the main, with the exception of some police leaders like James Mitchell in New South Wales, it was the police ministers, under pressure from the women's groups, who pushed through the changes. In Queensland, the first female member of parliament managed to persuade her cabinet colleagues to introduce women police. A very attenuated process ensued at the federal level and in the Northern Territory.

School road safety instruction, NSW Police, circa 1952.

Chapter 2

On the Job

The previous chapter showed that the campaign to appoint women police was, for the most part, conflicted and often protracted. With the exception of New South Wales and Tasmania, eventual success represented a triumph of perseverance and diplomacy on the part of women activists against a wall of ignorance and arrogance. Nonetheless, the introduction of women police quickly provoked further frustrations for the women police movement. While the 'experiment' of female officers was roundly considered a success — thanks in no small part to the quality of character of many of the first appointees — the promise of women police was never fulfilled. The new police remained locked into a narrow set of tasks related to women and children, in a highly subordinate position, confined in tiny numbers. This situated persisted up until the 1960s and 1970s.

Women's Employment Position

The employment position of the new women police varied considerably between jurisdictions. We saw in chapter 1 that the appointees in New South Wales bypassed the normal training system, were sworn in as Special Constables on a probationary basis for 12 months and worked in plainclothes. This was explained in part as an accident, in the sense that it was necessary to circumvent the rules because Lillian Armfield was above the designated age limit of 30 for appointment of officers under the Police Regulation Act. The women were on a lower pay rate than males. They were required to take out their own personal insurance, sign an indemnity releasing the force from any legal liabilities for their safety and agreeing not to make claims on the police pension fund. 'After thirty-four years of service Lillian Armfield retired without one penny being paid to her in superannuation.'[1]

In South Australia, the new officers were sworn in as constables. The Chief Secretary also announced that 'they will be treated the same as constables in regard to hours of labour and remuneration.'[2] Kate Cocks was given discretion regarding uniforms and she opted for plainclothes with a view to a less threatening appearance.[3] Nonetheless, the officers were issued with a baton, along with a badge, an identification card and a whistle. Higgs and Bettess described their employment conditions as follows:

> Each week the women worked approximately sixty hours and were allowed one day off every six weeks. Three broken shifts of 9 am until 1 pm and from 5 pm until at 11 pm were worked each week and in most cases the women were on duty at the same time. Seventeen days after commencing duty Annie (Ross) was granted special leave of half a day to shift house.[4]

One of the distinctive features of the South Australian system was that a separate Women Police Office was established, with accommodation in rented ground floor rooms at Victoria Square in the central business district.

In Victoria, Madge Connor and Miss Elizabeth Beers were sworn in without full police powers and in plainclothes. 'With no training and little more than a button to assert their authority, they jumped in at the deep end. Given the attitude of senior police, these women were brave.'[5] They were attached to the Plain Clothes Branch or the Metropolitan Police, under the authority of a Sergeant, and were issued with a detective's warrant card 'empowering them to extract information from all possible sources.'[6] They were allotted half the pay of male constables and were excluded from the pension scheme.[7]

In Western Australia, 'all the police department records relating to the appointment and function of the Women police from 1917 to 1927 have been destroyed and a list of prerequisites for their appointment does not exist.'[8] However, the Police Commissioner stated in the 1916/17 annual report that the women were 'sworn in as constables under the provisions of the Police Act, 1892.'[9] Helen Dugdale was a nurse and an 'Inspectress' in the State Children's Department. Laura Chipper worked for the Salvation Army in the Perth Rescue Home. By the mid-1920s, physical fitness and a background in nursing were made explicit criteria for appointment.[10] Nursing was most likely seen as inculcating discipline, and providing experience with persons in distress and persons suffering from mental illness. A nursing background also helped in control duties related to venereal disease.

Tasmania's first female officer, Katie Campbell was appointed as a 'Policewoman' but 'on probation.'[11] When she was discharged under mysterious circumstances three months later she was listed in the

Police Gazette as 'Constable (Mrs.) K. E. Campbell'.[12] Newspapers had reported that:

> The 'eight hour' day will be observed, and her work will be altered as circumstances demand. The uniform is blue walking dress, with badge and number attached, these distinctions of office for the time being having to be worn under the lap of the policewoman's coat. She will also carry a warrant card.[13]

The Mercury highlighted the lack of powers in the following report:[14]

> The local police force was enlarged yesterday by the addition of a woman constable, who is to take the place of the one recently resigned. The new officer will patrol the streets, and will undoubtedly be of great assistance amongst the female population, but she will have no authority to arrest, and in case of trouble she will have to "Call a Policeman." She will also attend the Police Court when female prisoners are being dealt with, and will render any assistance possible to them both before and after the hearing. When a woman or child is dealt with under the First Offenders Act she will look after their future, and give such advice as in necessary.

In Queensland, Ms Dare and Ms O'Donnell were appointed as probationaries in 1931, on a trial basis. They were not sworn in, had no police powers of arrest, and did not contribute to the police superannuation fund. There is no evidence that they received any formal training. They were issued with warrant cards, a form of identification used by plain clothes police.[15] A male constable started on 15s. 1d. per day. The new female officers worked for 9s. per day.[16] It appears they worked regular hours but with one on call out of hours. They were posted to Roma St Police Station in Brisbane's city centre, under the supervision of the Inspector for the Metropolitan Division.

The Commonwealth's first female officer, Constable Alice Liele Clarke, was appointed as 'a fully sworn member' in 1947.[17] A marriage bar applied. Of interest is the fact that 'policemen were issued with batons but policewomen were only issued with whistles'.[18]

Police Work

In his biography of Lillian Armfield, Vince Kelly, noted that 'in spite of the harshness' of her employment conditions, 'Lillian Armfield embarked on her duties with an enthusiasm that was sustained to the very last days of her service'.[19] She remained in the job from 1915 until retiring in 1949, aged 65. According to Kelly:[20]

It was a career that was varied and exciting. She became the confident of the wives and mistresses of the victims of murder. For those thirty-four years she was in daily and nightly contact with the seamiest side of Sydney's life. She understood and shared the heartache of parents and delinquent girls, and worked unceasingly to reclaim the girls themselves. Some of them were redeemed by her efforts, other died by the murderer's bullet, like Connie McGuire, others by suicide, like Nellie Cameron, or finished their lives degraded and unrepentant, like Mary Eugene.

She exposed charlatans, blackmailers, procurers, drug-peddlers, coiners, and during her long career she avoided publicity and worked as quietly as possible behind the scenes.

She said, "Some were vicious and dangerous. Some were just weak and easily led astray. The varying degrees of their wickedness made life for me always interesting, and often more than exciting, but I always felt that most of them had a chance of redemption and I tried to see that they got their chance."

A common task for early female officers like Armfield was to act as 'decoys' to obtain entry premises without a warrant on behalf of male detectives. According to Armfield, 'having served this purpose we were pushed into the background', and the male officers would make the arrest and process the offenders.[21] Drug dens were one type of location:[22]

My instructions were to avoid publicity as much as possible, and it was only when we appeared in court that that the public learnt about our work, and then only about those specific cases in which we gave evidence. So for quite a while it new nothing of what I was doing to help smash the drug traffic by gaining entry for police into opium dens, as a decoy to trap criminals, and my other work in suppression of serious crime.

In the apprehension of so-called fortune tellers, it was different. They had become a grave menace because of the war and the anxiety of people who feared for relatives at the front. There were cases of suicide reported to us to be due to the nervous strain some credulous persons suffered after consult-ing these frauds, who had flourished practically unchecked until we were used against them. We got so much publicity in our cases that against them that a lot of people assumed we were doing nothing else except trap fortune tellers.

In fact, the women's groups who had advocated for women police were unhappy with this line of work and expressed their dissatisfac-tion to the Colonial Secretary. The Minister reported that the women had been engaged in a much wider range of duties, including keeping children off the streets, particularly at night; patrolling wharves, train stations and parks to prevent young women being harassed or exploited by predators (including when women were 'leaving work in the evening'); patrolling 'slums' to intercept drunken women and provide support to their children; and engaging in charity-related enquires when it appeared appropriate to involve a police officer.[23] One of the duties reported by the Colonial Secretary was to peruse newspaper for advertisements designed to entrap young women. The findings were reported to male detectives to follow up.

All of the early women police, like many of their male counterparts, spent a great deal of time pounding the pavement on routine preventive patrols. They tended to have set routes covering parks, commercial districts, cinemas at closing times, and train stations when interstate trains were due. At stations they would approach women or young girls who had nowhere to stay or no means of support. This was designed to prevent rape, murder, abduction and procurement by pimps. With the same purpose in mind they would patrol wharves and meet ships. They would also walk through hotel 'parlors' looking for female under-age drinkers or women drunk and neglecting their children. Occasionally, while on patrol the women police would warn children about loutish behaviour or move on people causing a nuisance. Giving a warning, sometimes an emphatic warning, seemed to be sufficient in most cases to obtain compliance.

In South Australia, the women police appear to have adopted a strong welfare orientation, following up allegations of cruelty to children and abuse and neglect of children, intervening in family disputes, and even distributing welfare handouts such as clothes and rations. Higgs and Bettess report as follows on initial duties carried out by the new officers:[24]

> Hour upon hour was spent patrolling the Adelaide streets, Port Adelaide and Out Harbor wharves, beaches and parklands. Special attention was given to given to the Adelaide railway Station where there was always a large concentration of troops. Kate (Cocks) believed that 'it is a meeting place for girls and soldiers, and young girls parade about the station until they secure the attention of a soldier.'
>
> A quiet word to any unsuspecting prostitute or young girl loitering for an unduly long period was usually enough to send the ones scurrying home. As a preventive measure young girls were often escorted home and their parents warned to keep a stricter eye on them ...
>
> House of ill repute and 'cool drink shops' also came under close scrutiny. The 'cool drink shops' were a major worry to puritans concerned with the moral welfare of the citizens of Adelaide. Many were fronts for brothels but by selling small items such as cool drinks, cigarettes and sweets they allowed a large number of men into the premises without drawing too much attention.

The female officers would also conduct covert surveillance in what passed for a Red light District in the Sturt Street, and pass on their notes to male detectives who would conduct raids:[25]

> Louise Forster would delight her family when, with great gusto, she would tell of fleeing men, half-clad, clambering over high fences and leaping into the street hanging on to their undergarments. The women had a soft spot for the prostitutes and considered that the men were the source of evil.

However, in Adelaide, the women officers received the most notoriety for their work patrolling beaches, which were popular sites for amorous couples. Kate Cocks stated that, 'during the last few years it has become the fashion for couples to do their courting lying down', and the officers reportedly ordered couples to 'move "three feet apart, three feet apart"'.[26]

In the 1916/17 police annual report Kate Cocks reported on the work of the women officers as follows:[27]

Long distance trains met (147 persons assisted with accommodation, temporary monetary loans or escorted to homes of friends)	1,659
Steamers met (3 persons assisted)	79
Enquiries for other Government Departments (includes State Children's Department, Destitute Board and Public Trustee)	12
Girls rescued from immoral surroundings and placed voluntarily in institutions	43
Women placed in institutions	14
Women in distressed circumstances helped	65
Number of persons arrested and placed before the court (47 juveniles and 11 adults)	58
Absconders from State Homes arrested	6
Persons warned re conduct whilst on patrol	600 plus
Miscellaneous enquiries (include white slave traffic, suspicious advertisements, ill-treatment and neglect of wives by husbands, misconduct of wives — especially soldiers' wives with children, house of ill-repute, mentally deficient persons, aged, destitute and drunken women)	610

Assisting Criminal Investigation Branch	20
(in cases involving women — larceny, indecent assault, abortions, concealment of birth, fortune-telling and one coining charge)	

The extent of patrol work is illustrated in the following journal entries from 1926 by Louise Forster, the only female officer at Mt Gambier, South Australia. The entries also show that law enforcement could be a dull business at times. [28]

Saturday February 20th

2 pm	Patrolling streets and parks
3.30 pm	Attended Picture Show. Warned 3 small boys and 3 girls re their conduct
4 pm	Patrolling streets and parks
6 pm	
7 pm	In office
7.30 pm	Patrolling streets and parks until closing of Picture Show
11 pm	

Sunday February 21st

2 pm	In office. Later patrolled streets and parks
5.45 pm	
8.15 pm	Patrolling streets and parks
9 pm	Patrolled Railway Station. Met Beachport train and continued patrolling
9.30	Warned young camper re lying about the Park

Monday February 22nd

9 am	In office, writing etc.
12 noon	Patrolling streets and parks
to	
1 pm	
2 pm	In office. Interviewed Mr Sam Taylor re his daughter Florrie refusing to go to work. Florrie has been working at the woollen mills and is considered to be one of their best hands.

Patrol was often mixed in with follow-up visits on welfare or crime incidents. The welfare role is illustrated in the following journal entries, also from Mt Gambier, in 1941 from C.C. McGrath and M. Ottaway respectively.[29]

March 21st Thursday

9am	In Office

To Mrs Winifred Collins wife of Keith Collins, 28 and 29 yrs, res. 3 children. Received report Mrs Collins neglects her children and leaves them home alone at night, that she has numerous gentlemen friends. Denied all, but later admitted leaving her children home at night alone. Warned her. She is always with Rodericks etc. and out dancing late.

Patrolled Vausittart Park

Int. Mrs Brookesby re home conditions. Much better, she states that the children are better mannered and more obedient since my last visit.[30]

January 30th Tuesday

9am	In Office.

11am
In consequence of three complaints to the home of Mrs Pearleeu Victoria Peters neé Jones, wife of George William Peters, 27 yrs and 54 yrs res, Salvation Army. Four children, George William, 4yrs … John Richard, 3 yrs … Robert Bruce, 1 yrs … Alice Catherine, 7 mths … Rent 12/6 paid. The home consists of four rooms. The front bedroom, had a double bed and cot in it, unmade & indescribably filthy, the floor dirty, the room smelt. The 2nd room had a number of beds in it, the beds filthy, the children not taught any manners and had urinated on the floor. The 3rd room had a table and chairs in it, the floor was filthy the children having used the floor as a lavatory. The 4th room was the kitchen which was not as filthy but still dirty. The whole house had a dreadful smell about it. The children were dirty and their heads needed a bath. Warned both parents to clean the house within 24hrs or else the children would be arrested. Also to have the children clean.

Very occasionally the women had to deal with a sexual assault case, usually in providing assistance to the victim. There would be occasional arrests of a woman as a 'mental defective'. They would attend court sessions involving female accused or victims. The women police were sometimes called upon to provide domestic reconciliation services. This was the highlight of an otherwise dull day for C.C. McGrath in Mt Gambier, South Australia, on Monday 12th February 1940, as her journal entry attests: [31]

February 12th Monday

8AM   Mr Norman Wright called at my home address.
           Arranged to see him and his wife at 9AM.

9 am
Mr and Mrs Wright in office. Very little fault with Mr Wright only drunk on Christmas for 12 months, never struck his wife, always given her money. She seems very dissatisfied and in a bad temper, over nothing. He is away working all the week only home Sat. and Sunday. For two hours I pleaded, etc. with Mrs Wright and she will not return. Husband left her 30/- for board while she obtains a job. She's impossible.

General patrol

2pm   In office
           Journal
           Patrolled streets re school children

5pm   Off duty.

In Tasmania, the 1918-19 Police Department report provided the following description of the work of the two officers: [32]

> The work of the women police is carried out by Mrs. Hughes (Hobart) and Miss Cross (Launceston), and the appointments are more than justified by the results. A policewoman's duty extends much beyond the scope of work of the ordinary constable, inasmuch as she acts as guide, counsellor, and friend to all who, from destitute or unfortunate circumstances, need aid and advice. Where parents through drink neglect their children their homes are visited, with gratifying results. In numbers of cases suitable homes or situations have been found for girls on the way to become vagrants or worse, and many unmarried mothers who have been assisted and advised respecting their trouble. Good service has been rendered for the welfare of foolish or wayward girls idling in public reserves, in the suburbs, at railway-stations, wharves, and in the city generally. Useful work of a more definite police nature has been performed at the various courts, embracing the attendance of female witnesses, especially those of tender years, called to give evidence. This phase of the duties of women police has been most satisfactory. Policewomen escort female prisoners when travelling, which the latter much appreciate. The

policewomen have evinced ability, tact, and discretion, and thereby have secured the confidence and respect of the class they deal with. When the Children's charter is fully working I anticipate increased duty for the women police; in fact, I have recommended that they be appointed probationary officers under the Act. The women police do good work respecting truancy, which police experience shows is the first step to crime.

A grateful parent had the following Letter to the Editor published in *The Mercury*, under the title 'Lady Police':[33]

Sir.—Notwithstanding woman's alleged inferiority to man in all callings ... The lady-police in this city have already proved that that they are endowed with finer brains and intelligence in dealing with and preventing crime than are the majority of their brother officers in their work. Although only forming a sideline in their work, allow me as a father, to applaud their successful methods of dealing with schoolchildren who are habitual truants. In six months their kindly judicious advice has worked more good in this respect than all the sledge-hammer bullying bluster of male officers. Keep to your good work ladies! Parents appreciate you!

Leonie Stella's account of the early years of women police in Western Australia is less sanguine. She claimed that the assistance women police were supposed to provide to women and girls in difficulty was, in fact, moralistic social control:[34]

This 'welfare' work was in practice surveillance of women, particularly young women suspected of being 'immoral' and likely to spread venereal disease. Although the women police did carry out welfare duties which protected and assisted some women and children, particularly neglected children, the restriction on their duties together with the fact that they were primarily appointed as 'morals police' resulted in them interfering in the lives of working class women rather than assisting those who were victims of sexual crimes committed by me.

Stella's observed that the early appointees:[35]

were white anglo-saxon protestant women ... trained to work in the field of nursing and 'rescue' work. They carried out their duties in a manner which indicated they were 'the right type of woman': women with the religious moral values dominant among middle-class women of their time, possessing a strong 'air of authority', and some nurturant and compassionate qualities. They believed that in, in dealing with 'wayward girls', neglected children and 'immoral' women, it was necessary to reform, protect or 'rescue' them for 'their own good'. They were selected to be 'morals police' and considered to have the attributes appropriate for such a role.

The threat of venereal disease amongst the troops made potentially contagious women allegedly a key target of the new officers. Stella assembled some limited evidence of their involvement of this form of surveillance and control. Legislation obliged the officers to arrest women under the age of 18, suspected of having a venereal disease, under charges of being 'neglected', 'incorrigible' or in 'moral danger'.[36] This would allow the arrested girl to be subject to a health examination. The girl could also be placed into state care. Stella also cites cases of the women police separating couples considered to be too close to each other in public places. However, a good deal of her descriptions of the women's work indicates a strong primary focus on the wellbeing of women and girls. In addition, in her earlier account of the development of women police in Western Australia, Sandra Sinclair described how during the Great Depression women police acted to some extent as scouts for welfare agencies in identifying individuals and families most in need of emergency assistance.[37] This included emergency accommodation following evictions.

In Queensland, the new officers, belatedly appointed, had similar duties to their interstate compatriots. Escorting female prisoners, sometimes on long train journeys, was a periodic assignment. On occasions they were required to search female prisoners, although this was not a regular task. The police retained a 'female searcher' in the city watchhouse. Other duties, described by Commissioner Ryan, were typical of the role assigned to policewomen at that time:

> Interviewing women in connection with sexual offences, acting as Police Agents in obtaining evidence against fortune tellers, etc., shadowing suspected persons, making general inquiries regarding women and children, attending Courts and escorting females and children to and from the Courts when necessary.[38]

Ryan noted that the women had been successful in securing evidence to obtain convictions in several cases, although he remarked that their work in taking statements was confined to juveniles. He appeared pleased with the 'experiment':

> The two Probationary Policewomen have carried out their duties in a very satisfactory manner. They are not yet fully experienced, but are ener-

getic in the discharge of their duties, and I consider they have justified their appointment as an auxiliary unit of the Police Force.[39]

Women police in Queensland appear to have had somewhat more of a law enforcement focus than in some other states, although this did not involve controversy as in New South Wales. The Queenslanders paid more attention to shoplifters and abortionists, with a view to prosecutions, and may have spent more time in court both as witnesses and when women and children were accused. Queensland's first female officer supposedly held a record for catching 120 shoplifters in one year and this part of her work received media attention when she retired in 1965. *The Courier-Mail* reported that, 'Once, to trap one of Australia's most notorious handbag thieves, Miss O'Donnell spent hours posing as a customer in a city store and trying on scores of hats. She left her own handbag nearby and caught the woman red-handed as she snatched the handbag'.[40]

The Movement for Expansion and Equality

Police Commissioners were almost always positive about the police women's work. Sometimes they were quite effusive. In the 1930s, the Tasmanian Commissioner reported on the work of the only female officer in the State, based at Hobart, in the following terms: 'Splendid work has been effected at Hobart for the welfare of foolish or wayward girls idling in public reserves, about wharves, railway stations, and in the city generally'.[41] However, this enthusiasm rarely extended to increasing the number of female officers. In Tasmania there was a woman officer in Hobart and one in Launceston until 1922, when the Launceston officer resigned. The northern half of Tasmania had to wait until 1940 before another policewoman was appointed to Launceston, with an appointment at Burnie on the north coast in 1944.

As noted earlier, within a short time of the first appointments of female officers, women's groups in Sydney were frustrated with the direction of their work. They were not satisfied by the Colonial Secretary's account, nor were they satisfied with his lack of commitment to increased numbers. Mrs Annie Golding, President of the Women's Progressive Association, complained publicly that the new officers were simply serving as assistants to male officers rather than acting independently in a preventive role to divert women and girls from crime and harm.[42] The women's groups also felt that the female officers were being used to arrest and punish female offenders when the male co-offenders, and likely instigators, were ignored.

Mrs Golding summed up the latter problem as follows:

> Girls are still being apprehended in immoral houses or in rooms with men by the police-women, and also for soliciting, and they are charged and remanded to Long Bay Jail or summarily convicted. And they are being dealt with in just the same way as policemen dealt with them, and in just the same way the keepers of such premises and the men concerned go free, and in the same, bad old way the woman has to bear the whole brunt — odium, conviction, and loss of liberty.[43]

A public outcry followed the arrest of a girl by Armfield and a male officer on a charge of being 'idle and disorderly'. The girl had been apprehended in a park where, according to welfare workers, she had merely spent some time after looking for work. The girl also had accommodation with her sister but was remanded in Long Bay. She appeared in court with her hair cropped and, with her agreement, was ordered by a magistrate to reside in a religious home for six months. Women's groups were outraged over the whole process, while Armfield defended the arrest, arguing the girl was in an unkept state and that her hair was 'verminous'.[44]

In another incident, Armfield arrested a girl who had been associating with a man known to have venereal disease. The man was sent to Long Bay Jail for treatment. The girl was held on a charge of vagrancy and at the hearing police advocated for the charge to be dropped and the girl discharged into the care of her mother. However, the mother and the girl's solicitor successfully fought the charge and the arrest was widely reported in the Press as oppressive policing.[45]

Disillusion with the role of the women officers in Sydney led to proposals to remove the police designation and change their title to 'vigilance officers, or something less misleading than policewomen'.[46] Commissioner Mitchell rejected the idea, although Armfield reputedly offered to resign to save him the ongoing controversy. After Mitchell rejected Armfield's offer and encouraged her to persist, she reportedly asked for more female officers. However, Mitchell's support did not extend that far.

South Australia presents a somewhat different picture. In April 1916 the *Register* reported that the government was 'so impressed' with the work of the women police that a decision had been made to appoint a third officer. Mrs Mary Wilcher, a 35-year-old nurse and a widow, was appointed in July. Two more appointments in 1917 made for an 'invincible quintette', as male colleagues called them. The enlarged numbers forced a move into an adjacent building where the group occupied both floors of a two-storey house, allowing for the creation of five interview rooms.

All was not well, however, on the issue of pay, and in 1918 the women officers resigned en masse with their male colleagues in a dispute with the government over pay and conditions.[47] The Chief Secretary refused to meet with the new Police Association, necessitating the appointment of a private arbiter. Mary Wilcher provided testimony:[48]

> Her salary was 9s 6d a day plus an annual uniform allowance of nine pounds. After paying house rent of 15s a week, child care for her son of 5s a week, plus electricity, food and other household expenses she only had 10s a week left to purchase clothing and other incidentals. She also pointed out that the work was arduous and extremely heavy on clothes and in particular on shoes. The increases sought by the Association would have meant that Mrs Wilcher who had been employed for two years by the department would have been entitled to an additional 1s a day in salary plus 1s a day in lieu of quarters.

The arbiter recommended a pay rise but recommended the women officers receive 1s per day less than the male officers. The Association successfully argued that the women had been appointed 'on the same terms as the men', and after further negotiations women were granted the same increase as the men.[49]

These issues were repeated across the country.[50] Victoria was a telling case in point. In 1920, two of the women police and a group of watchhouse matrons bravely sought a meeting with the Chief Secretary Major Baird to explain their financial plight. The women outlined the often extreme and unpleasant nature of their duties, shifts between 14 and 16 hours per day, and the fact their pay did not cover the amount needed to 'live decently'.[51] Madge Connor pointed out that the women police had to pay for their meals when working outside the station, that they received no pension, they had to pay for their own clothing — which was expensive to ensure a respectable appearance — and that they still did not have full police powers. The deputation was successful in obtaining a pay increase, but the rate remained well below that of a male constable. Mrs Connor tried for a further pay rise in 1922. Her petition included the signature of the Chief Commissioner. The women's supervisor, Sergeant Matthew Campbell, wrote in support. Some success was achieved through the addition of a uniform allowance.

Madge Connor was persistent. She tried again in 1923. With the support of Sergeant Campbell, and the Superintendent of the Melbourne Police District, the petition for equal pay was successful and applied from January 1 1924. The petition included the following personal account:[52]

> There are only three policewomen in Victoria, and to increase our allowance by the same amount as it proposed to give some of the married men would add very little to the Department's expenditure.
>
> Speaking personally I am a widow living with my two daughters, and my rent alone is 30/- per week. Our pay and allowances at the present time amounts to 10/6 per day, but with the cost of rent, living and clothing I find it extremely difficult even with the strictest economy to make ends meet. In fact I am not always successful in so doing.

Throughout the 1930s, the number of policewomen in Queensland remained at two. Commissioner Ryan reported that in 1933 there were approximately 1,262 male police officers in Queensland. The two women made up slightly less than 0.15% of the total number of officers at a time when Queensland had a population of approximately 950,000 and Brisbane had approximately 300,000.[53] In 1933 the NCWQ wrote letters to the Commissioner noting that it had come to the Council's attention that the women did not have equality with policemen and did not contribute to the pension fund. The Council politely suggested that equality was preferable and that the good work done by the women justified an increase in their number.[54] Ryan replied that:[55]

> It is the policy of this Department to rank such members as supernumeraries; they were advised of the conditions when they were taken on, and signified their approval of such conditions. They may resign at any time if they wish, if they are not satisfied.

Ryan's replacement, Commissioner Carroll (1934–49), was lukewarm towards female police. When the NCWQ and WCTUQ lobbied for equal standing he argued that the two incumbents were unsuitable for permanent status, apparently on the grounds that they were too old (Ms Dare was 51 and Ms O'Donnell 41).[56] He subsequently met with a delegation from the NCWQ and promised the group that he would give the matter further consideration[57] but took no action.

World War Two

The Second World War reproduced many of the social conditions of the first, with male workers recruited by the military and soldiers and sailors flooding into portside areas, with concerns about venereal disease and wayward girls. Women's groups renewed their lobbying efforts in favour of more female officers.[58] In this context, the South Australian Women Police Office provided a model for a distinct unit of female officers, followed by Queensland, while elsewhere the war provided an opportunity for some expansion of the numbers of women officers and a large volunteer auxiliary force in Victoria.

In Queensland, Zara Dare married in 1940 and was obliged to resign from the Force. Elizabeth Boyle was appointed in her place. O'Donnell remained at city station with uniformed police while Boyle was posted to the Brisbane Criminal Intelligence Branch (CIB). A decision was made to introduce more formalised training for her and subsequent appointees. However, most of the women appointed during the war did not receive any training.[59] In Brisbane, the large influx of US servicemen contributed to an escalation in elopements and domestic disputes, and the situation generated something of a moral panic and a call for more control of young women.[60] The type of concerns that led to the expansion of policewomen's work is evident in a request made to the Commissioner by the Brisbane Women's Club:

> The Civic Sub-Committee of the Brisbane Women's Club wishes to recommend the appointment of additional policewomen to restrain the conduct of young women towards the members of the fighting forces on leave in the city. It is felt that the present number of women police is insufficient to cope with the situation, and that many young men are enticed into undesirable company because of lack of supervision in the vicinity of hotels.[61]

In this case, the main concern appears to be for protecting the troops. In other cases, protective concerns regarding sexual assault and unwanted pregnancies were focused more on women.[62] Policewomen were deployed in surveillance work in places such as the notorious 'love pit' in the National Hotel in central Brisbane which had a floor show on the ground floor and a brothel upstairs. The floor show area attracted many under-age girls. The 'passion pit' at the Grand Central Hotel was another hot spot to be surveyed for missing girls.[63] Policewomen were expected to keep a low profile and they had little direct contact with servicemen. If force were required, then male police would be called in. The women had very little to do with organised prostitution, which was handled by detectives in the Consorting Squad, probably in association with graft.[64] The women's work was also extended to include assistance in the control of sexually transmitted diseases. The Consorting Squad picked up suspected female carriers and took them to clinics for examination.[65] Policewomen were required to be present during examinations to prevent sexual abuse and reduce the subjects' resistance. The process was 'as automatic as ring a doctor and ring a policewoman'.[66]

Commissioner Ryan had described Queensland policewomen informally as an 'auxiliary unit'.[67] But rather than create an official auxiliary, it was decided to create a sub-unit within the CIB. The Commissioner and Minister agreed that more policewomen were needed and the Minister announced that a staff of four women was planned, with further additions in the future.[68] Accordingly, Miss Boyle was appointed as 'Supervisor, Women Police' by the Commissioner in June 1941.[69] She was directly responsible to the Inspector in Charge of the CIB. Commissioner Carroll personally selected most of the other women appointed during the war.[70] The Police Women Section began as Boyle, Alison Johnston, appointed in 1941, and one advertised vacancy. The section was attached to the CIB which was housed in a badly leaking former church, several blocks away from the Roma St Station.[71]

The typing load of detectives appears to have been an added factor in the push for more female officers. The police restricted the use of civilians for clerical duties because of concerns about confidentiality.[72] A letter from the Commissioner to the Minister in 1940 makes it clear that the women's role was envisaged as a dual role of operational police officer and stenographer to male investigators. From that time, advertisements always emphasised a thorough knowledge of shorthand and typing. In 1956, in an equal pay case, it was noted that Queensland was the only state where these skills were required by policewomen.[73] One former officer recalled that 'it was nothing to be chained to the typewriter for a month'.[74] In the mid-1950s it was estimated that the women spent 40% of their time typing for detectives or commissioned officers, although they did not perform clerical duties.[75]

Eight additional women were appointed in Queensland during the war. With resignations, the total staff of the section numbered nine in 1945 and remained around that level for the next 20 years.[76] The end of the war did not occasion any apparent reduction in the perception of the need for policewomen but there were also very few calls for increases. Commissioner Carroll had an extremely narrow and traditional view of the role of women. Nonetheless, the policewomen saw him as a supporter and their employment remained as secure as it could. Subsequent commissioners were seen as largely indifferent towards the section, but indifference also meant that a degree of security was assured.[77]

During the war, Carroll had been able to have the approved strength of the Police Women Section increased to twelve,[78] but the quota was never filled. Boyle wrote numerous memos outlining the problem to the head of the CIB, who passed them on with supporting comments to the Commissioner. Advertisements for the vacancies were usually approved, and the understaffing was attributed to lack of suitable applicants. The labour shortage produced by war and post-war development was a likely factor.[79] The pool of likely candidates was also greatly reduced by the narrow age band of 25 to 35 years, as well as a height limit, marriage bar, and bar on divorcees and single mothers.[80] Changes to these restrictions were never apparently considered. The attrition of policewomen when they married also kept numbers down. 'There was no question of staying on after marriage', recalled one woman forced to resign in order to marry.[81]

In Queensland, as elsewhere, the work itself was highly varied but far from the full range of police duties. There were occasional postings to different sections such as Modus Operandi, or with the Licensing Branch checking unlicensed premises and sly grog dealers.[82] Women continued to work in plain clothes, and did regular hours with one woman on call at night and the weekend. Staff on call generally stayed in their homes and would be picked up by car if needed.[83] The public response was usually respectful and co-operative. If anything, 'people were intrigued. There was a lot of mystique.'[84] Policewomen were of course a very rare phenomenon in Brisbane. 'People never knew what to say to us and they used to say, "Are you a policeman woman?"'[85]

Some states responded to the increased demands on women officers during the war by creating volunteer female police auxiliaries. It was felt that police status was unnecessary for the tasks assigned to auxiliaries for the war's duration (such as clerical and switchboard duties, and driving vehicles). Ten 'honorary police women' were appointed in Western Australia in 1942,[86] while a larger group developed in Victoria. At the federal level, women were employed as Peace Office Guards, to guard commonwealth buildings, from 1942. According to Osborn,[87] the number of female 'POGs' peaked at 345 in 1943.

Woolley reports that in Victoria, 'a total of 202 women served in the Women's Police Auxiliary although there were never more than 61 at any one time'.[88] Unlike the women police, the auxiliary officers wore a uniform, eliciting some confusion about their powers and responsibilities. In Victoria, they were engaged as 'clerks, typists, switchboard operators, drivers and receptionists, releasing for active work men who formerly carried out these duties',[89] and were placed under the authority of Senior Constable Kath Mackay. Chief Commissioner Duncan enthused that they 'have proved themselves more suitable than men'.[90] The number of women police had reached only 12 by 1944.[91] The auxiliary system was continued beyond the end of the war in 1945, and in early 1946 a proposal went to Cabinet supporting their paid employment on a lower rate of pay to males as a cost saving measure. Cabinet agreed but the proposal was not implemented, possibly because of union opposition and opposition from Kath Mackay. The work was really public service work and bore no direct relation to regular 'police' work. The women's auxiliary was eventually disbanded in 1953.

Queensland: 'The Equal Pay Fiasco'[92]

According to Rod Eddington, Queensland Police Union of Employees President from 1963 to 1977, Inspector Tom Lloyd of the CIB 'initiated (the policewomen's) application to join the union so they could get equal pay'.[93] The women were admitted into membership in October 1955 following a decision at the State-wide conference held in March of the same year. The motion was carried unanimously.[94] Some policewomen, at least in the 1940s, saw their salary as much better than they could obtain in other occupations, including the public service.[95] In 1940 the pay rate was determined departmentally as that of a probationary constable. After 12 months service, increments were paid every five years for twenty years. In 1950, it was decided to determine the women's salaries according to those of female clerk typists in the State public service; with allowances such as plain clothes, rent and week-end penalty allowance, and an adjustment upwards of seven years given the higher age entry requirement. This appears to have produced an improvement, although the policewomen's rate fell markedly behind that of public service clerk-typists in the next five years.[96] The altered schedule was a separate arrangement to a general pay rise for police in 1950.[97]

Following a conversation between O'Donnell and the Union General Secretary in August 1955, the Union executive decided to pursue an industrial award for the women.[98] A case was heard in the Queensland Industrial Court the following year. The Industrial Acts provided equal pay for men and women for the same work; and the union case extrapolated the women's duties and length of service to the rank of constable, and equated the supervisor's position with that of a senior sergeant. The fact that women performed shorthand and typing was not seen as particularly significant given that male cadets were trained in these skills.[99]

Police Commissioner Glynn opposed the Union's submission and sat through the entire proceedings. Mr Tait, for the Public Service Commissioner's Department, on behalf of the Police Department, argued that the women could not be considered equal to policemen. The women had not undergone proper training and had not sat for promotional exams. They were not sworn members. They did not wear a uniform. They worked fixed hours and were not subject to transfer. They undertook substantial amounts of typing and had duties more 'akin to those of a welfare worker'. The Union's claim was deemed 'extravagant and unreal'.[100] Commissioner O'Malley of the industrial court concurred with most of the Union's arguments. A 'substantial increase' was ordered, which amounted to 80% of constables' or probationary constables' wages depending on length of service. Given that women were not rostered for weekend work, weekend penalty rates were discontinued.[101]

Following the conclusion of the hearing, the police Commissioner lodged an objection, arguing that the relevant industrial Act did not specify women as employees of the police. The commissioner argued that the women were employees of the Department of Labour and Industry — the police portfolio — and that therefore the court had no jurisdiction.[102] The Union immediately made a lengthy submission presenting a wide variety of evidence to show that the Commissioner had previously acted on the presumption that policewomen were his employees. Amongst other things, annual reports listed the women as part of the full strength of the force and the women's warrant cards identified them as 'a member of the Queensland Police Force'. However, the Commissioner's objection was simply ignored as coming too late.[103]

O'Malley left the parties to decide upon the details of some matters in conference where the Commissioner maintained his opposition to being designated as the employer of policewomen. The matter came back to the industrial court and the President of the Court, L. Brown, found in favour of the Commissioner on the grounds that the women did not take the oath of office required for membership of the police force as described in Section 14 of the Police Act. Brown deemed that the policewomen were employees of the permanent head of the Department of Labour and Industry.[104] The Police Award — State was varied to clearly identify policewomen (and police cadets) as employees of the Department of Labour and Industry but now subject to the specific provisions of the Police Award. A 'Policewoman' was defined as 'any female employed to perform any class of Police duties or to assist members of the Queensland Police Force in their duties'.[105]

The Press were quick to comment on the uncertainty arising from the case. The *Telegraph* ran an article under the headline 'Women Not in Police Force (Court told)'.[106] Boyle and Police Woman Ryan attended the hearing and had their photograph attached to the *Telegraph* report. Following the ruling, the paper suggested that there was now a question mark over the power of policewomen to search women who had been arrested and that the women might be guilty of impersonating police officers.[107] The *Truth* asked, 'If they're not (police), are their tram passes any good? What about jobs they do, like handling marked money or traffic breaches?[108]

There is no apparent record of any great alarm amongst police over the allegations. The feeling may have been that the definition of policewomen now written into the Act was sufficient to give them legitimacy. The women had always been careful to request permission before searching bags, and body searches were conducted under the direction of a sergeant.[109] All the same, *The Courier-Mail* reported that the minister, Mr Jones, indicated that it might be necessary for at least some of the women to be sworn in.[110] However, Jones' role came to an abrupt end when the Country-Liberal coalition took power in August 1957 and the ministry changed hands.

Conclusion

For many decades, the appointment of women police in Australia represented something of a Pyrrhic victory. The battle to allow women into policing was won, but the war for equality was lost. Male decision-makers in politics and policing had grudgingly made a very small space for women, but the new officers were then hemmed in on all sides. For the most part, the women were busy, and like most of their male colleagues they worked long and exhausting hours for meagre pay. The new officers acquitted themselves with great aplomb, but their field of endeavour was confined to stereotypical 'feminine' tasks and they were very much under the control of male officers. The following chapter charts the beginnings of the breakout from this narrow space.

Chapter 3

Breaking Out

This chapter takes up the story from the 1950s as social change enlarged opportunities for women police. Heading into the 1960s, the global women's liberation movement provided a further impetus for female police to start to break out of their confined and subordinate roles. Across Australia's eight jurisdictions there was a protracted and halting process which saw the gradual erosion of established norms around the duties of women police. Key milestones included equal pay, equal powers in New South Wales and Queensland, removal of quotas and the marriage bar, and integration into the regular rank structure. Women police units were shut down as female officers went out on patrol and served alongside their male colleagues as nominal equals. Police unions increasingly supported the case for equal treatment of female officers. Maternity leave became available. More and more women police were assigned outside capital cities. Female detectives were appointed. By the 1980s, something of a revolution was apparent, with an established profile of female officers in uniform on the streets and in squad cars. However, closer examination showed the revolution was far from complete. A patchwork of barriers remained, including variable quotas on the proportion of female officers. Notional equality also meant being locked into full time work, with little or no consideration for family responsibilities — either for males or females. The idiocy of discrimination was especially profound in Queensland, where wildly shifting polices and the mistreatment of women officers receive in depth treatment in this chapter.

Road Safety: New South Wales and Queensland

In the post-World War Two period, the rapid growth in automobile use resulted in an expanded role for police in traffic control. In 1947, New South Wales Commissioner William Mackay returned from an overseas trip enthusiastic about the role of female officers in road safety education with children.[1] The Commissioner called for volunteers and Amy Millgate and Gladys Johnson were assigned to the Traffic Branch. The women had been in the military, and they designed uniforms based on World War Two models. The experiment was considered a success. A School Lecturing Branch was established in 1951. 'By 1962, over half of the 58 female police special constables in NSW were attached to the School Lecturing section, talking to students about road safety.'[2]

In the 1950s, the idea appears to have caught the attention of the new Queensland Police Minister, Mr Morris. One of his first actions was to announce the creation of a 20 strong unit of uniformed policewomen to work at school crossings and give road safety lectures to school children. The rationale of relieving policemen for other more pressing duties was brought out; this time, 'to meet the recent demand for more intensive policing of the suburbs'. It was also noted that the new unit would focus attention on child welfare work. '"Copettes" soon in City Streets!', the *Truth* announced.[3]

Opening the Door: Equal Powers in New South Wales

The marriage bar on continuing employment was lifted in New South Wales in 1961 as a result of a 'departmental decision to permit women to remain in employment ... after marriage'.[4] On March 18, 1965, women police in New South Wales finally achieved equal powers.[5] The officers were sworn in by Commissioner Norm Allan at a ceremony in the auditorium of the CIB Branch in Surry Hills. They also obtained long service leave, equal superannuation entitlements and access to the pension and, it appears, equal pay. These achievements have been attributed in part to evidence about the extent of the women's work presented by Special Sergeant Joan Weaver, Officer-in-Charge of the Women Police Section.[6] In addition, officers in the CIB lobbied the Police Association executive to petition the Police Commissioner in support of equal powers.[7] Female officers had been admitted into membership in New South Wales in 1947, following repeated requests from the women.[8] No doubt, the campaign was helped by the fact the size of the female police complement. By the mid-1960s, there were approximately 60 female special constables in New South Wales.[9]

A number of anomalies remained, including a separate seniority list which confined women to competition among themselves for promotion, thereby severely limiting their promotion prospects.[10] However, equal powers provided the catalyst for the initiation of equality across a range of other employment conditions. The first women to qualify and be appointed as detectives were Gwen Martin and Del Fricker in 1971.[11]

Melinda Tynan observed that 'the apex of this period of change came in 1976 with the transfer on a trial basis of four women to general patrol duties'.[12] Clair Britton was posted to the Mascot Airport police station. Christine Nixon, Margaret White and Christine Ridley were assigned to Darlinghurst Police Station, reputedly the busiest station in the state, located in the heart of Sydney's red light district. At Darlinghurst, the women met considerable resistance from a police culture that was notoriously corrupt and violent.[13] Their sympathy for female victims of crime and female offenders, including prostitutes and drug addicts, disrupted the self-interested routines of male officers and challenged their insensitive handling of complex and delicate matters. The women's integrity did not win them a lot of friends, and they had to assert their right to do the same work as men. However, their perseverance and competence ensured they prevailed, and another 'experiment' with women police was deemed a success.[14] Their pioneering work led to a policy, in 1980, of women police going directly into patrol work after being sworn in. The Women Police Office was closed in 1981, and the integration of women into the regular seniority list occurred across 1978-1981. Despite these developments, the quota on female recruits was only removed after a very brave Victoria Carr took action in 1980 against the Police Force before the Anti-Discrimination Board, established as part of the new 1977 Anti-Discrimination Act. In 1981, Elaine Thompsett was successful in having the Board outlaw the marriage bar in recruitment.[15]

The Journal of Women in Policing published a summary of key milestones in New South Wales in a 2013 historically oriented issue of the journal. Some additional milestones to those that have been outlined earlier — including one very tragic loss — are as follows:[16]

- By 1979 firearms became standard issue for policewomen and Gwen Martin was the first women appointed to the Executive of the NSW Police Association.
- Jill Frazer received the Policewomen of the Year Award for bravery. She died from injuries after being assaulted by an offender during an arrest. In 1981 the Equal Employment Opportunity Branch was established at Police Headquarters and began to assist women with discrimination and harassment issues.
- Constable Sally Verhage became the first police woman in the Police Rescue Squad (1981).

- Constable Lisa Ford was certified the first police woman diver in 1984 and went on to become the first woman in the Water Police in 1986.
- The first woman appointed as patrol commander Bev Lawson, became the first women superintendent and district commander and later deputy Commissioner.
- Detective Inspector Lola Scott was appointed the first women patrol tactician at Redfern in Jan 1993. The following year she became the first women detective chief superintendent when she was appointed Commander Internal Affairs and the first to be appointed as Region Commander in 1997.
- In 1994 Constable Debbie Lee became the first police women appointed to the Police Dog Unit.

Developments in Other Jurisdictions

A similar pattern of change ensued in most of the other Australian police departments, with police unions increasingly acting on behalf of women police. It would seem that collegial relations between the sexes on the job made union members amenable to policewomen's rights and to union membership. One exception to the usual adversarial process of change was South Australia. There was very little change until 1974, when internally driven modernisation processes led to the disestablishment of the Women Police Office, women were put into uniform and mixed patrols, the marriage bar for continuing employment was lifted and seniority lists were integrated[17] In 1977, women were allowed to carry a firearm. In 1979, women were permitted to join the cadet courses and the first female commissioned officer, Fay Leditscke, was appointed. In 1982, Sue Vivian was the first woman appointed to the Mounted Cadre, and in 1983 Kathryn Finnigan became the first female Detective Sergeant.[18] In a sign of the times, in 1984 The Police Wives Association in South Australia changed its name to The Police Partners Association.[19] In 1984 the South Australian Police Association journal included an article reporting that, 'There is considerable evidence that women actually make better police officers than men'[20].

In Victoria, the third state to appoint women police, major changes were signalled by a 1971 review of the force by Eric St Johnson, which recommended an enlarged role for women police.[21] In 1972, married women were allowed to join. Numbers increased and in 1973 most female officers were moved out of the women police units and put into various departments under control of the officers in charge. Maternity and paternity leave were granted to police in 1975. Female officers joined the Mounted Police and Fingerprint Bureau. The Equal Opportunity Act came into force in 1978, prompting the integration of seniority lists and the assignment of the first women to general duties. In 1982 the Women Police Divisions were disbanded. They were replaced by 'Community Policing Squads', which were open to male and female officers while retaining a somewhat feminised welfare oriented role. The day of 20 April 1986 was a dark day in the history of women police in Victoria, when Constable Angela Taylor died from wounds received in the bombing of the Russell Street Police Headquarters.[22]

The Australian Federal Police (AFP) was established in 1979, incorporating the Commonwealth Police, Australian Capital Territory Police and the Federal Narcotics Bureau. There were 195 female officers continuing in the new force covering a wide range of duties including general police duties in the Australian Capital Territory, investigations, juvenile aid and protective security.[23] According to Delia Quigley[24]

> In the mid 1980's Melita Zielonko put forward a case to the Human Rights and Equal Opportunity Tribunal, which gave AFP women the right to be able to serve on Peacekeeping missions which had previously been a male domain. The Australian Federal Police has given women the wonderful opportunity to partake in such missions since 1988 when Kathy Burdett was the 1st AFP female to serve in an overseas mission when she was a member of the 28th and 29th AUSTCIVPOL contingents to Cyprus.

In Western Australia, female applicants to the police no longer needed to be trained nurses from 1960. In 1975, the officers were issued with uniforms — 'albeit complete with gloves and handbags' — and the marriage bar on appointments was lifted. In 1976 women began training at the Academy and the Women Police Section was disestablished.[25]

Women were only appointed as police in the Northern Territory in 1961. According to the 1960/61 police annual report:

> The first policewomen to be enlisted in the Force commenced duty during the year. These members are performing a multitude of tasks and have proved themselves to be very valuable additions to the Force. It is quite apparent that the present staff of five policewomen is inadequate

and it would appear that a staff of seven policewomen at Darwin and three at Alice Springs will be required in the near future.[26]

The late-stage appointments meant the women were given full powers and equal pay from the start. However, they were still expected to resign when they married. In 1969, a list of women who had resigned and the reasons for resigning was compiled.[27] Between 1961 and 1969, of 33 women who resigned, 13 left due to 'marriage'. Three left because of conditions in the male barracks where they lived. One of these wrote, 'Cannot live under conditions in Barracks for rest of career in Force'. Another referred to an 'inability to adjust to juvenile values in my environment'. A number found the climate and lifestyle in the Territory too demanding.

The closure of women police units marked a turning point in the removal of a major marker of separate status. The units were closed in the Northern Territory in 1967, Queensland in 1972, South Australia in 1974, Western Australia and Tasmania in 1976, New South Wales in 1981 and Victoria in 1982. Many of the women in these sections were opposed to their closure. They felt comfortable in the limited role that they were able to make the role work for them.[28] Jean Priest was one the women police philosophically opposed to integration. After she joined the Tasmania Police in 1923 she was the only female police officer for 13 years and was proud of the fact she never made an arrest:

> When I had to start finding people who were breaking the law, like the widow who was selling from her shop illegally, on a Sunday, I resigned … I just wanted to help people. I wouldn't want the job of a policewoman now, it's nothing like it used to be.[29]

Table 3.1 shows the dates of achievement for various key milestones including equal pay, uniforms, integration into the rank structure, closure of the women police sections, removal of marriage bars and mixed patrols. In 1968, the census recorded women as 1.2% of police officers. They made up1.8% in 1971, 3.7% in1976, 5.8% in 1981, 9.4% in 1986 and 11.9% in 1991.[30]

Struggles for Equality in Tasmania

In Tasmania, one young woman's annoyance at different standards in recruitment set in train a series of events that resulted in equality in the entry age. As late as 1977, the Tasmanian Police could advertise

Table 3.1 Summary of Milestones in the Establishment of Women Police in Australia

Milestone	NSW	VIC	TAS	SA	WA	NT	QLD	C'wealth
Appointment	1915	1917	1917	1915	1917	1961	1931	1947 (ACT)
Equal powers	1965	1924	1917?	1915	1917	1961	1975	1947?
Equal pay	1992?	1924		1915	1917	1961	1970	1947?
Uniforms	1948 (trial) 1951	1947	1973/74	1974	1976	1978	1965	1968
Rank	1947? 1964?	1956? 1971?	1917		1917?	1977/78	1965	
Closure of women police section	1981	1982	1976	1974	1976	1967	1972	1974?
Removal of marriage bar (continuing)	1961	1972	1970	1973	1975?	?	1971	?
Removal of marriage bar (recruitment)	1980	1972	1972	1973	1975?	1967?	1971	?
Maternity leave	1975	1975	?	?	?	1976	?	1976?
Paid maternity leave	1975?		1993?	?	?	?	?	?
Mixed patrols/ general duties	1976 (trial) 1980	1978	1976	1974	1977	1978	?	1973

differing recruitment requirements for men and women, as shown in the following newspaper advertisement.[31]

Tasmania
POLICE

The high-grade,
well-paid career with GO!

* First year Constables start at $8,499 pa *

For Men: Well educated, physically fit, no aids to eyesight, minimum barefoot height 175 cms. Aged 19 to 33.

For Women: Same basic requirements. Aged from 22 to 42, minimum barefoot height 157 cms.

Ex-Servicemen! Join within two months of service discharge and LS Leave counted as Police LS Leave.

Pity the poor male wanting to join the police who was too short at 174.5 cms or over the hill at 34! But males could join the force as cadets, studying school subjects, as young as 16.[32] In 1976, the Tasmanian government embarked on an unemployment reduction plan focused on school leavers that included expanding the number of places for male police cadets from 38 to 68. Advertisements were placed in newspapers. The Premier's Adviser on Women's Affairs received several complaints from young women,[33] which included the following impassioned plea.[34]

Flat B/63 Giblin St.,
BENAH VALLEY. 7008

6th July, 1976

Mrs K. Boyer
Women's Adviser to the Premier,
Public Buildings,
Franklin Square,
HOBART. 7000

Dear Madam

On Monday 5th instant I was talking to a lady from the Commonwealth Employment Service and she suggested I write to you to see if you could help me with my problem.

After three years of careful thought and consideration I have decided to become a Policewoman. I went into the Police Careers Office for some information and pamphlets concerning my future career. Needless to say the wind was completely knocked from my sails when I was told I had to be 22 years of age before I could join the Police Force. As I will be 19 in August I feel three more years of waiting will seem like a lifetime.

I feel I am mature enough to cope with almost anything which may arise during the course of my duty. With the training I'm sure I could be a competent Policewoman.

I regard it as being most unfair that women must wait until they are 22 and men may enter as a Cadet at the age of 16–17 years when it is a scientific fact that women mature earlier than men.

I am sure I am not the only person who wants so desperately to become a Policewoman at 18–19 years.

When the age of consent was lowered from 21 to 18 I thought that this would have applied to joining as a Policewoman.

Could you please forward my comments on to the Premier and Members of Parliament for the consideration of lowering the age for women to join the Police Force.

Hoping for a prompt reply.

Yours faithfully.
JANET HULCOMBE. (MISS)

Kim Boyer did some homework and took action, beginning with a memo to the Minister for Police recommended equality in ages for entry. The memo was forwarded to the Police Commissioner who rejected the proposal. The Minister accepted the Commissioner's arguments. Ms Boyer then appealed to the Premier, in the following letter.[35]

9th November, 1976

THE PREMIER

I refer to one of the points in your 24 point plan to reduce unemployment, that offering additional police cadetships for the Police Academy.

As you probably know, this will only help male school leavers. The recruiting age for the Police Force is 16–23 for males and 22–42 for females.

I believe, this would be an appropriate time to reconsider the female police recruiting age, and indicate the government's real concern for unemployed female school leavers, as well as eliminating discriminatory employment practices.

At present there are many more unemployed female school leavers than male school leavers in Tasmania. The CES figures at the end of October, was boys 227; girls 321.

The main argument which has been used against lowering the female police recruiting age is that women are more mature and have had time to try other occupations by the time they reach 22. No one would dispute that; but the comment could apply equally to boys.

For your information, I understand that the Rokeby Police Academy is quite willing to have female cadets.

The Commonwealth Police Force has the same recruiting age for males and females — 19–40.

I believe, this could be a popular issue in indicating —

(1) The Government's concern is for both female and male unemployed school leavers.

(2) The Government is committed to elimination of discrimination against women in employment.

(Kim Boyer)
ADVISER ON WOMEN'S AFFAIRS

Ms Boyer's intelligence and diplomatic logic contrasted sharply with the narrow self-interested reasoning of the Commissioner in his earlier correspondence with the Minister.[36]

14th May, 1976

The Minister for Police
The Honourable B.K. Miller, M.L.C.
C/- Attorney-General's Department,
HOBART.

I refer to your memorandum of 7th May 1976, forwarding a copy of a memorandum from the Special Advisor on Women's Affairs.

The reason we stipulate the age of female recruits as being twenty-two years is that we have no difficulty in obtaining suitable recruits in that age group. Whereas for males we have found it unnecessary to recruit Cadets at the age of sixteen years before they take up any other occupation. After two years cadet training they can then be sworn in as a Constable at the age of eighteen years.

I think that the age of eighteen years for a female is too young to accept the responsibilities of a Constable. However, this is my personal opinion and I have recently received a comprehensive report from the Victoria Police which deals with all aspects of the employment of Policewomen. This report is to be discussed at the Commissioners' Conference next month. After the Conference I will report to you on the integration of Policewomen into general Police duties, age of recruitment and other matters affecting their employment.

(E.V. Knowles)
COMMISSIONER OF POLICE

It would seem that the report referred to was the US Police Foundation report *Policewomen on Patrol.*[37] This was an innovative study conducted in the District of Columbia Police Department in 1972–73 that compared the performance of male and female patrol officer on a wide range of measures. The conclusion was that on most measures women were as good as men. Women also seemed to be better at diffusing conflict and were less prone to misconduct. However, the Police Commissioners' conference was unable to agree on a policy, with some maintaining their concerns about women's ability to handle violent situations. Ms Boyer was informed by the Police Minister that Tasmania would continue to recruits women at 22, 'as applicants are more mature and are more likely to continue with a Police career'.[38] In a newspaper report on the issue Commissioner Knowles elaborated on his views regarding 22-year-old females:

> They have got stability in them then, they know whether they want to be old maids, so to speak, and they know how to protect themselves...

> There are lots of opportunities for girls in typing, stenography, and as clerks with the force...
>
> They are more suited to that particular area at a younger age and really of more value to us.
>
> It's certainly not discrimination.[39]

The archival correspondence on this issue is incomplete, but suddenly a new Minister, Eric Barnard, wrote to Ms Boyer in 1978 declaring that women cadets would be recruited at the same age as males as soon as female showers and toilets were completed at the academy.[40] The precise role of the key actors here is uncertain — Commissioner, Minister and Women's Adviser — but when *The Mercury* reported that the age limit for the swearing in of females constables had been lowered from 22 to 19, equal to males, it was explained as 'part of the Government's policy to remove sex discrimination'.[41]

Many women who pioneered the way for today's women have retired or resigned with a sense of bitterness and unfulfilled potential. This was illustrated in a special report by *The Saturday Mercury* in Hobart in 1996. A journalist interviewed five of the most senior women police and a retired Inspector. Some said that they had never experienced any discrimination, but this appears to have been an uncommon experience. The experiences of Sergeant Wanda Miller appear more typical, especially of those who spoken out against unfair restrictions in the period of the '70s and '80s where policing careers were only half opened to women:[42]

> Some policewomen give up because they can't see any point trying for promotions they're not going to get, says Sergeant Wanda Miller.
>
> The officer in charge of Smithton police in Tasmania's far North-West, Sgt Miller, 44, said she had to work 'three times as hard as any male,' to reach her position.
>
> "I have not been given the equivalent relieving opportunities as my male colleagues," she said.
>
> "I speak for myself alone."
>
> A former officer in charge of the scientific section in Launceston, Sgt Miller transferred to Burnie about two years ago to take up the position of personnel sergeant.
>
> After she sold her house in Launceston and moved to Burnie, the position did not become available. She was given the option of working as a shift sergeant in the uniform section, transferring to the country, or transferring back out of the district.
>
> 'I chose Smithton. The position at Burnie never got off the ground, yet is was a proper gazetted position that I applied for'.

Despite being eligible to sit for her inspector's exams since 1992, Sgt Miller decided to go no further up the ranks:

"I've made a conscious decision not to do my inspector's exams because I don't consider I've been treated well over the past few years," she said.

"I've fought for policewomen's rights from the beginning and to that end I've been labelled a potential trouble-maker. But if it hadn't been for me and policewomen like me, the policewomen of today would not have got the clear run they have.

It's been to the detriment of my career because I've been too outspoken."

Sgt Miller was the dux of her training course and dux or equal dux on other courses including drug investigation, breathalyser, traffic law and advanced driver training. Despite holding a motorcycle licence, she said that she was denied access to the motorcycle training course in the late 1970s.

Sgt Miller said that when she joined in 1977, policewomen were not allowed to wear trousers in the daytime, making it necessary for them to walk the beat in skirts, stockings and high-heeled shoes.

"I wasn't happy with that and that was one of my first sorties offering my opinion," she said.

Sgt Miller said that she once had aspirations to get to the rank of inspector 'but I can no longer see light at the end of the tunnel. I'm burned out'.

Sgt Miller said that young policewomen have it much easier in the 1990s.

Another furphy was that women police wouldn't be accepted by the community. This was an especially good excuse for keeping women out of country stations. Heather Innes 'applied to be officer-in-charge at 12 country stations before she was finally accepted. 'I was not allowed to take on a country station because I was single and there were concerns that the community wouldn't accept me'.[43]

Removal of the marriage bar in Tasmania had an easier passage. In 1970, the Northern Branch of the Police Association requested that the Executive ask the Commissioner to consider allowing women police to stay on in the job after marriage.[44] The Executive agreed and the Commissioner agreed. He stated, "I am prepared to allow Policewomen to continue to serve after marriage and have already approved of this for two members."[45] From that time the marraige bar was effectively removed for serving female officers, but it is not clear if the Commissioner had originally planned this as general policy or had merely permitted two women to continue as ad hoc decisions.

In Tasmania in the late-1960s and early-1970s there was a sustained campaign to have a female police officer appointed permanently to the West Coast Division, which included the frontier-style beat of the mining town of Queenstown. Women police visited the area on average three days every quarter. There was support from the Divisional Inspector, a local politician, women police, the Child Health Association and the Country Women's Association of Tasmania. However, the Deputy Commissioner resisted, arguing that most of the women's work could either be done by men or was welfare work that should be done by Social Service Department.[46]

Equal Powers: Queensland

In Queensland, the issue of equal powers took the better part of a decade to resolve. The matter came to the fore in the 1950s with the Minister's plans to put uniformed women police at school crossings. The question of a new unit included the issue of swearing in and the Deputy Police Commissioner advised Commissioner Harold on the feasibility of the move. Some possible complications were envisaged regarding different retirement ages and physical requirements. A prohibition on married policewomen would also have to be written into the Police Acts and Rules. 'For obvious reasons they should not be married', observed the Deputy. It was also suggested that women would have to be excluded from the superannuation scheme. Apart from these considerations, the Deputy appeared to favour making amendments to include women in the force — subject to the advice of the Solicitor General.[47]

The legal advice was that the Police Acts were exclusive to men and that a new Act was needed specifically for women. Commissioner Harold recommended this course of action to the minister, and also supported the idea of a new separate unit. It was felt that most of the existing policewomen were too old and not up to the physical standards needed for the proposed unit.[48] Harold retired soon after in December 1957. Twelve months later *The Courier-Mail* reported that 'equality may soon rear its pretty head in Queensland's police force'.[49] The paper reported an announcement by Bischof, the new commissioner, that he would soon make recommendations to Morris regarding the employment of more women. An expanded role was muted, especially with traffic duties: 'The women would release men "for more masculine duties"'. The fact that policewomen earned four-fifths of a policeman's wage was seen by Bischof as a major inducement to women to apply to the force.

Bischof had become Officer-in-Charge of the CIB in 1955 after working as a detective from 1933.[50] He worked closely with many of the women and this experience appears to have disposed him somewhat favourably towards their work.[51] One woman who worked in the 1950s suggested that Bischof saw policewomen as 'a necessary evil'[52] but, from the perspective of another, 'Frank Bischof was for policewomen'.[53] The two views were a fairly accurate reflection of the equivocatory attitude expressed by Bischof in different forums and of his procrastination on gender issues. In September of 1959 Minister Morris wrote to Bischof chiding him for not replying to four requests for responses to Morris's recommendations.[54]

In March 1958 the WCTUQ wrote to the premier urging that policewomen obtain 'the same standard as the male with all the powers',[55] and the issue of the uncertain legal standing of police-women was revived in 1958 when the union agreed at a conference to recommend equal powers for policewomen.[56] The potential for civil action against the women was uppermost in the arguments made at the conference.[57] The union approached the commissioner who asked the CIB for advice. Early in 1959 the Inspector in charge of the CIB wrote to Bischof recommending that the women be properly inducted. He suggested that they stood in danger of civil action for assault, especially in carrying out searches, and that the only reason that any aggrieved parties had not taken action was because they assumed the women had equal powers. "I do consider that the time has arrived," the inspector wrote, "when Policewomen should be put on an equal footing with members of the Force in so far as their statu-tory powers are concerned."[58]

In correspondence with the minister, Bischof continued to pro-crastinate. He stated that for some time he had been considering giving the women full police powers and putting some into uniform doing traffic patrol near schools. He had also given consideration to allowing the women attached to the CIB to follow investigations through to court 'in suitable cases'. He acknowledged that these changes would require amendment to the Police Acts and entail enhanced training. He then suggested that change of this extent could impact adversely on a proposed campaign to attract more applicants to the vacant positions. He thought that the adoption of a uniform might aid the campaign but felt that the other changes should wait until the section was brought up to strength.[59]

In October 1959 the minister approved Bischof's plans for a publicity campaign to attract more women but action was deferred because of budget restrictions.[60] In 1961 the union reiterated its support for swearing in policewomen and for giving them uniforms.[61] In 1962 Bischof ordered a review.[62] A submission was made to Minister Pizzey in 1963 advocating amendments to the Police Acts to allow for women to be sworn in, and arguing for equal pay and superannuation.[63] Pizzey showed little interest until further prompting from Bischof and a member of parliament, John Herbert.[64] In October 1963, Cabinet approved Pizzey's submission for amendments to the Acts but action was deferred because of uncertainty over details. All but one of the policewomen were over the age of 30, the age limit for swearing in, and none had received formal training. Some of the women approached the Union expressing concern about possibly being overlooked. Police Woman Olwen Doolan had walked down George Street to parliament house to put the same concerns before Herbert, her local member.[65] Bischof declared that protection of the status of the existing policewomen was uppermost in his mind, and a compromise was eventually sorted out which allowed the women to be sworn in with supplementary training for all — excepting Boyle and Frisch, the two most senior women.[66]

As with the initial appointment of policewomen, final action to swear in women appears to have depended on action by a member of the government; although in this case it involved support and some initiative from the commissioner. Alex Dewar took over from Pizzey in 1964 and encouraged Bischof to press on with the details of legislative change in time for the next sitting of parliament.[67] In August of 1964 Dewar won approval from Cabinet and in December he introduced the Police Acts Amendment Bill to parliament. The Bill included changes to the police appeals system regarding promotion and punishment.

The amended legislation also allowed for pension rights for the women. Benefits were to be calculated at a slightly lower rate than those for men. Compulsory retirement was set at 60, the same as for men. Dewar also announced his intention to gradually increase the number of policewomen and gave voice to Bischof's vision of a greater role for women in road safety and in the Juvenile Aid Bureau. Plans were also announced to put women into uniform and to introduce training in law. Entry was set at 23 to 30 years of age. (By then, male cadets were taken at the age of 17 and sworn in at 19.) Dewar indicated that the age limit of 23 was designed to recruit women fairly well confirmed as spinsters. If the age were lowered, he argued, 'We could go through the process of training them and swearing them in, and then lose them'.[68]

Bischof failed in his bid for equal pay for the women. The Labor opposition were fully supportive of the amendments, but immediately seized on the continued inequality in wages. Dewar took the advice of the Public Service Commissioner on pay rates and insisted that the issue was the province of the Industrial Commission. The opposition argued that the government should ignore the commission and take the opportunity to set a major precedent for equal pay for all women. It was claimed that the policewomen would be doing essentially the same work as policemen and should therefore be paid accordingly. Mr Houston argued that if the minister had a tooth extracted, 'he would not expect the dentist to charge less because she was a female'. Dewar responded that policewomen would not be expected to perform, or be capable of, the full range of police duties. 'I do not think any hon. member or any body in the Police Force would envisage sending these girls out to do the jobs done by men. They will not be required to get dead bodies out of the river or to quell riots. There are dozens and dozens of jobs these girls will not have to do'. Mr Bennett, for Labor, countered that the women would nonetheless be engaged in work 'more revolting and distasteful to their finer feminine feelings than the tasks that women are normally called upon to perform'.[69]

Following the passage of the Act, the eight serving policewomen were inducted on 31 March 1965 in a special ceremony before the Commissioner and the Minister at the training centre at the Petrie Terrace Depot. Supervisor Boyle became a Sergeant and the other women were given the rank of constable. Four new appointees began the probationary course a week later and three were inducted in uniform on 30 June. One of the appointees had dropped out following a visit to the morgue.[70] By 1966 there were nine women in plain clothes and four in uniform.[71] The female officers began to make arrests, mainly for minor crimes such as shop lifting. The traditional strategies of 'cautioning, advising and assisting' were maintained.[72] Swearing in did gave the women more independence from detectives and they were able to operate much more as free agents. The Women Police Section obtained a car, which further facilitated their independence.[73] The uniformed women were more likely to have to deal with street offences but they were usually in the company of males.

When women were inducted in 1965 there were two women in the Juvenile Aid Bureau, which grew steadily in the second half of the 1960s. Women made up to one third of staff, and men and women worked in pairs whenever possible. There was a strong sense of equality and camaraderie.[74] 'There was a wonderful atmosphere', one woman recalled who worked in the Bureau for 19 years. The Officer-in-Charge, Terry Lewis, is attributed with creating an environment that was 'totally supportive' and he appears to have encouraged Bischof to expand the Bueau and, consequently, the number of policewomen.[75] Some stereotypes persisted. For example, male and female teams would tend to play 'tag team' in interviews. The male officer would take the more threatening approach and the female officer the more caring approach.[76]

Equal Pay: Queensland

In 1969 the Queensland Police Union revived the issue of equal pay. It wrote to the Commissioner arguing that women could be put into the full range of duties and that this would assist the case.[77] Commissioner Bauer inquired into the possibility by surveying district officers. The officers felt that women were being deployed to the virtual limits of female ability. At the same time, they wanted more women for traditional tasks.[78] Bauer promised the Union that 'as opportunity offers, the work of Policewomen will be extended to cover all fields of Police activity'.[79] At a District Officers' conference in 1970, concerns over the continued attrition of women due to marriage led to the suggestion that the entry age should be lowered. Bauer obtained the support of the minister to lower the age to 21.[80]

The Union had made a concerted effort to obtain equal pay in 1956, in a complicated and protracted legal case. It had tried again in 1964 when the decision was made to give women equal powers. Further submissions had been made to the Industrial Court in 1966 and 1967.[81] The Industrial Court had power, from as far back as 1917, to grant women equal pay on the basis of equal work, but it repeatedly accepted the argument that the work of policewomen was less demanding than that of policemen.[82] At the 1970 union conference, executive member Ron Redmond moved that the Union 'take all possible steps to obtain equal pay for Policewomen'. Redmond stated that he had been directed by members in the CIB 'to forcibly put this matter to you for consideration'. He also noted that 'Policewomen feel that they have a just right and they are justly annoyed that they have not been given consideration'. The remark suggests that some lobbying by women in the CIB may have been behind the motion. Redmond argued that although policewomen did not 'fight bushfires, quell riots, do rescue work in floods, etc.', the segmented nature of police work meant that women performed specialist work of equal value within the totality of police tasks. General Secretary Callaghan supported the motion and Mr McMullen recounted an incident in Rockhampton in which a policewoman broke up a brawl. The motion was carried with no objections.[83]

A plaint for equal pay for women was included in a large pay claim filed with the Industrial Conciliation and Arbitration Commission of Queensland in July 1970. Kathryn Harper, who had worked as a police officer in New South Wales before joining the Queensland police, gave detailed evidence favourably comparing the duties of policewomen in Queensland with those in New South Wales — where equal pay obtained. Pat Ryan, in charge of the Police Women Section, also testified at length about policewomen's range of duties.[84] The Commissioner's advocate opposed the claims and argued that policewomen were not generally expected to control crowds, 'overpower violent men', take charge of stations, ride motorbikes or direct traffic.[85] Ray Whitrod, who took over from Bauer as Acting Commissioner, suggested that the Union should find out the situation in other States, and it appears that the suggestion was made as a way of improving the case for equality.[86] The Commission agreed with most of the Union's claims, including the argument that policewomen were now doing work equivalent to men's.[87] On the first of September 1970, 39 years after the first policewomen were appointed, equal pay was finally achieved.

The Deep North: The Whitrod Years

In Queensland, the 1970s saw two major changes in fortune for women police under two very different commissioners: Whitrod and Lewis. Commissioner Ray Whitrod was appointed in 1970 from outside Queensland to drag the Force into the twentieth century. Up until that point, women made up less than 1% of sworn personnel in the Queensland Police, slightly below the national average. During the six years when Whitrod was commissioner, policewomen numbers increased rapidly to a peak of 8.5% of sworn personnel. Whitrod claimed that in 1976 women were 10% of police personnel (a figure that probably included recruits) and that this was the highest percentage in the Western world.[88] Whitrod was directly responsible for opening the recruiting process to women by accepting female applications as a matter of routine and encouraging selectors to take on women. In 1970, six women were sworn in. The numbers then increased to 11 in 1971, 89 in 1972, 67 in 1973, to 109 in 1974.[89]

The move to recruit more women was initially prompted by a shortage of suitable male applicants. Women were recruited because they were better qualified than male applicants and suited Whitrod's goal of 'procuring intelligence': 'They were not appointed because they were females. It was a recruitment policy to get the best possible person'.[90] Nonetheless Whitrod went beyond merely opening the doors for women. He vigorously defended the expanded program, especially in his fortnightly newsletter where he reported on developments in the employment of policewomen in Australia and overseas. He congratulated policewomen whenever they excelled in various aspects of police work, using the cases as examples of the equal capability of women.[91]

During 1973–74, Whitrod made strenuous efforts to recruit Indigenous women. After failing to find any interested adults he sought younger applicants who could come in as cadets. Following extensive inquiries six Aboriginal women aged around 17 and 18 began in a special section of the academy. A Deputy Matron from the Brisbane General Hospital was employed to care for the recruits' special needs. The scheme fell apart for a variety of reasons: homesickness, inability to adapt to routine and, in one case, a pregnancy. Whitrod saw the failure of the idea as a significant disappointment.[92]

By 1974 there were 216 sworn female members of the force (up from 22 in 1969). In 1975 there were 26 female probationaries at the academy and 67 female cadets.[93] In some places the presence of women was very noticeable. Townsville, for example, at one stage had 20 or more young policewomen.[94] By the end of 1972 there were policewomen in Cairns, Bundaberg, Mackay, Rockhampton, Toowoomba and Southport as well as Townsville.[95] In 1973 there were 31 policewomen working in Brisbane mobile patrols. Of these, 29 were trainees.[96]

Apart from expanding female recruitment, Whitrod introduced other changes favourable to women. He removed the marriage bar, disbanded the Police Women Section, and integrated women into regular squads and into the one seniority list. Whitrod's removal of the marriage bar appears to have been prompted initially by a letter, written by a policewoman, outlining the wastage rate of women due to marriage, and passed on to the commissioner by her supervisor.[97] Whitrod had a strong interest in victimology and established a rape squad staffed by women to provide a more sympathetic response to rape victims. The creation of the squad meant that female members could obtain the necessary training and experience to interview rape victims and give evidence in court.

The State Public Service Acts, amended in 1969 to allow for the employment of married women, did not apply to the police, and the high resignation rate of women due to marriage prompted Whitrod to seek an end to the marriage bar. Hodges put the amendments through cabinet and parliament in October 1971.[98] In effect the changes allowed for the re-appointment of women upon application to the commissioner. Resignation or automatic dismissal still applied when existing policewomen married. Accouchement leave was included in the changes and the recruitment age was lowered to 19, with a maximum age of 30. Women were also allowed to enter as cadets at 15 (beginning in 1972). The changes were designed, in the commissioner's words, to 'make a career with the force for females far more attractive'.[99] By 1974, 30 of the 183 policewomen were married; 19 of these were married to policemen.[100] In August 1972 the Police Women Section was disbanded and most of the women were assigned as plain clothes officers to different areas of the CIB such as Fraud

Squad and Drug Squad. There were no formalities nor fanfare and, apparently, no tears were shed.[101]

One of the many 'firsts' for policewomen in the Whitrod period was the appointment of Noala Holman as officer in charge of a one person station at Woody Point in Brisbane in 1971 — also reputed to be the first such appointment in Australia. In reality, Holman was at the desk from 9-5 to allow a male officer to attend to outside duties.[102] Nonetheless, her appointment caused disquiet in the area. A local councillor was particularly perturbed.[103] According to Whitrod, the councillor:

> jumped up and down and created a few political waves. He wanted a man there. He couldn't understand how a woman could carry on that job although it was one mile from a divisional police headquarters with a 24 hour team on mobile duty. So he had a history of being, I think, an Olympic sportsman, and I arranged for Constable Holman to go and call upon him and pay her respects. And when he found out that Holman had been four times the Australian international goalkeeper for women's hockey he modified his opposition instantly and we had his support thereafter.[104]

Whitrod made integration a policy but left final decisions about postings and rosters to district officers. After over a century working almost entirely with their own kind, male officers were suddenly faced with a new type of partner. According to Whitrod, there was widespread resistance to the policy.[105] Discrimination took various forms including pejorative comments, lack of co-operation and differential assignment. As one woman recalled:

> There was a lot of reluctance to even work with women. When we first went to the station the natural response from the senior sergeant was to put you straight on counter duties where you issued licenses and took reports and lost property... There was a feeling that women couldn't do the job properly. We weren't as strong, we couldn't run as fast, we couldn't drive as well.
>
> *So that was communicated?*
>
> Yes. A lot of the men had an opportunity to choose between a male and a female partner. They'd pick the male partner. That was fairly common, even the female officer doing the late shift would be at the station doing some typing or answering the phones while her partner was out in the car.[106]

Most women were obliged to assert their right to equal treatment: 'If you were prepared to say, "Look give me a go on the street", they probably would look at it'.[107] A common form of discrimination was over-protection — often well intentioned, but discrimination nonetheless: 'I remember being in the CIB, and it wasn't because they were negative towards me it was that protectiveness. If there was something going on: "well look you go and interview the female" or "stay in the car" or whatever because there were firearms involved'.[108] Whitrod had to push repeatedly for officers to put women onto the same duties as males.[109]

Many of the women interviewed for a study on women in the Queensland Police during this period felt that women had an edge over men in managing conflict. The following story about an incident involving a two woman patrol team in Queensland typifies the way many interviewees felt about the physical ability issue.

> There were two females in the car and the car was directed to the brawl in the carpark. We walked up to them and the two fellows fighting turned around and looked and saw two females and said 'Oh oh' and stopped. And we said, 'Can we have a chat to you?' And they said 'Okay' — because it was a shock to see two women get out of the car and nobody else and then when back up arrived it was really interesting to see the shock on their faces. We said, 'It's okay fellas. We've got it under control'. That was really interesting. But, yeah, brawls most men go to tend to be over by the time you get there anyway ... I don't think there is a problem and in fact if there was a problem you'd get back up anyway.[110]

The Queensland Police Union continued to advocate for the appointment of policewomen to all district headquarters to work with women and girls.[111] It also lobbied for policewomen to be allowed to do casual work for other departments and for promotional vacancies to be open to men and women.[112] But by 1972 the union was anxious about the number of women being recruited at what it saw as the expense of males. There was also growing anxiety about women in patrol cars and on night duty.[113] Many rank and file officers felt that equal pay should mean equal work and did not mind handing over some of the unpleasantness of night duty to women.[114] Union President Ron Edington was less enthusiastic. He was reported in the press as saying that there was a crime wave caused by lack of male officers and too many 19 year old 'Ainsley Gottos ... joining the force on $4,200 a year to buy their trousseaus'. Whitrod was accused of hiding staffing problems 'behind policewomen's skirts'.[115] Edington subsequently claimed that he was quoted out of context.[116]

Apart from the presumption that policewomen were meant for office duties, in Queensland female probationary constables also had to contend with various forms of sexual harassment. Interviewees from that period were unanimous in saying that sexual harassment was generally of a minor nature, although its effects ranged from irritating to distressing. It appears that most perpetrators were easily dissuaded when women resisted: 'Others used to just cop it and go home and cry in frustration because they weren't going to say anything and get badmouthed around the station'.[117]

Male police were not the only group concerned about integration. Some policemen's wives also had fears, which they communicated to their husbands: 'Some of the men weren't working with policewomen, not because they had any objection, but because their wives were concerned that something might happen with a male and female officer together out in a car'.[118] A small number of wives of mobile police officers expressed concern about their husbands being on night duty with young women. The issue received newspaper coverage under the banner, 'Scandal brews over prowl car police girls'.[119] Some policewomen were also concerned that too many females were entering the force. They felt that women should stay in small numbers in a protected specialised role.[120]

Sources tended to agree that discrimination was not a significant problem at the academy (which opened in 1972). Most emphasised how a strong feeling of camaraderie developed between all recruits and staff. One interviewee had a different view of academy life, but felt that it was difficult to separate ill treatment in gender terms:

> Everybody, regardless of gender, got treated pretty badly if you ask me ... the PE area was a bit of a problem. We had some lunatic there once who sent a squad running around the perimeter of the academy... just before lunch on a summer day and they had males collapse. Actually, in that squad none of the women collapsed but several of the men collapsed and were carted off in ambulances for heat stress. That person was quickly transferred out of the academy.[121]

Criticisms reached Whitrod of the female recruits' supposed inability to manage physical confrontation and he invited critics to the academy to view the cadets in training:

> Luckily, we had the Tubman twins out there. One was in fact the judo champion of Queensland at the time. And whenever possible I emphasised the Tubman prowess as an example of how women could be taught to be more physically powerful than they were; although I always accepted that they cannot really match a man... except that our women

cadets were in much better nick than some of the fat old sergeants who spent their days either riding around in a car or boozing up.[122]

It appears that by 1976 a rough quota of two women per squad of 25 had been established with a view to stabilising the number of policewomen at 10%. With women then making up 8.5% of sworn personnel (302 of a total strength of 3,549), they made up 12.6% of probationaries and cadets.[123] A policewomen deputation to Whitrod also resulted in an important symbolic change in the removal of the official term 'policewomen' and the title 'PW'.124

Whitrod resigned suddenly near the end of 1976. He had had a constant battle with the police union and the government over his modernisation policies and his idea of the independence of the office of commissioner.[125] Whitrod's resignation was viewed by many women with dismay:

> People like myself and other people who came in as cadet women at that time believed the rhetoric of Ray, that he was there to create a professional police agency … And then when he bailed out prematurely, as I saw it, he left us to the wolves. I met one of Ray's other friends at a conference and she said, 'Have you met him?' I said, 'No, but I've suffered because I was allegedly considered one of his supporters'. That was bizarre because this is someone I'd never even met … but, nevertheless, in the Lewis years I was considered one of Whitrod's princesses … and I said to this woman, 'Look I'm not sure when I meet him whether I should hug him or hit him'.[126]

The Deep North: The Lewis Years

In the late-1950s the Queensland Police were dogged by corruption allegations centred on a group of officers known as 'the rat pack'. It was alleged that membership of this group included Terry Lewis. From his posting in the country, Lewis cultivated political connections of sufficient strength to enable him to be promoted to Commissioner upon Whitrod's resignation in 1976. With Lewis supporting the conservative Bjelke-Petersen government on law and order issues, the police were left unaccountable in many areas of administration.[127]

In the area of gender equity, the most obvious damage done in the Lewis years was the decimation of policewomen numbers by cutbacks in recruitment. Figure 3.1 shows the change in the percentage of policewomen in Queensland from well above the Australian average in 1976 to well below the Australian average a decade later. Sources vary, but numbers fluctuated somewhere between a peak of approximately 8.5% in 1976 to 5.2% in 1989.[128] At the time, two categories of trainees were recruited: probationaries and cadets. Probationaries were over 18 years of age and completed a short training program. Cadets were recruited directly from school and completed between one and three years of training depending on when they left school. In 1978 the recruitment of female cadets was halted. The quota of two per squad of 25 was maintained at probationary level. At times, two women per 50 men were recruited.[129] Continuing attrition of serving officers meant that female numbers were not being adequately replenished.

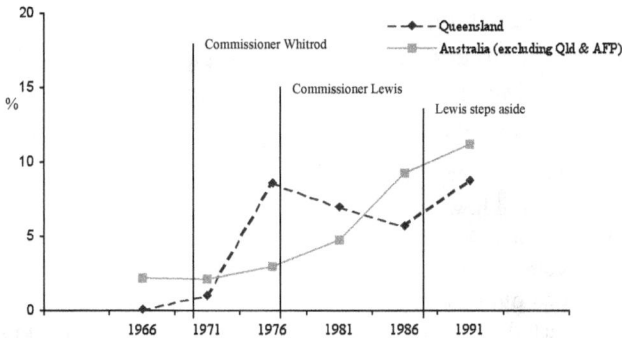

Figure 3.1
Percentage of Women in Australian Police Forces and in the Queensland Police, 1966–1991.[130]

In 1977, the Planning and Research Branch of the Force produced a report on policewomen which showed high drop-out rates.[131] The average length of service for policewomen was 2.24 years. Marriage, starting a family and 'personal reasons' were commonly cited reasons for leaving. (Accouchement leave was only six months.) For many of the years that female resignation rates had been an issue, there were also claims of high male resignation rates,[132] but the two were never compared. All the same, it appears that the report was read as showing that training women was a poor investment and that this was used as a rationale for reducing the number of female recruits.[133] Most females making enquiries about recruitment were dissuaded from applying by a lack of encouragement. A female officer was attached to panels interviewing female applicants. One of these panel members recalls the unpleasant experience of rejecting large numbers of women: 'Some kept coming back all the time'.[134]

Lewis's fixation with policewomen is apparent in diary entries made over the duration of his administration. One entry made within the first year of his assumption of power stated baldly: 'Policewomen integration not really successful'.[135] Another entry in the same year stated: 'Conference — discussed no need for P/W in Water Police'.[136] The commissioner requested regular statistical reports showing the declining number of policewomen,[137] and he rejected requests for women to be posted to one person stations, stating that he thought that policewomen did not have the same role as policemen.[138] Despite the fact that the orders for the cutbacks apparently came from Lewis, there is a question about the degree to which the policy was his own. Whitrod has suggested that another alleged member of the Rat Pack, Tony Murphy, may have had an influence:

> I'm not sure how genuine Lewis's hostility to women was. You'll know that as soon as his elder daughter reached recruitment age he then immediately started recruiting women and she served a short time before being invalided out on a handsome compensation payout. I don't think Terry Lewis acted very much on his own. I think he's very much dominated by his peer group, that is the rest of the Rat Pack. I think that Murphy was clearly the leader of that team and I think that over the years they'd grown up accepting Murphy as the principal guiding officer.[139]

The influence of the police union was also a likely factor. Union hostility was a major factor in the demise of Whitrod, and Lewis was quick to make peace with the powerful group.[140] Although Lewis did not restrict policewomen's duties to the extent that was demanded, the cutbacks placated the union on the issue.

One of Lewis's more notorious actions was a 'terror campaign' in 1978 involving the interrogation of policewomen about lesbian relationships.[141] Tony Murphy and another senior officer investigated an alleged 'lesbian cell' of policewomen who purportedly openly displayed their homosexuality in Brisbane nightclubs.[142] At least seven women were interviewed about their sex lives:

> *What do you know about the witch hunt?*
> Well I was friends with a few of the girls who got persecuted.

So they were interrogated as to their sexuality?

Yes interrogated, threatened.

Threatened in what way?

Threatened to have the issues exposed to their families.

Any other threats?

No, they were the only ones that I am aware of. They were told that they were going to be transferred, and to accept the transfer and not create a fuss, otherwise their family would get to hear all about their sexuality.[143]

It appears that the threats of transfer and disclosure were designed to intimidate women into resigning and some women did resign rather than be transferred away from their partners. The next best option for the inquisitors was to use transfers as a way of breaking up relationships and a number of women were transferred out of Brisbane. It is not clear that any family was told that their daughter was a lesbian, but some of the women were provoked by the inquiry to tell their families.[144]

From October 1977, Lewis's diaries contain a number of cryptic references to the investigations; for example:

Saw A/C McIntyre re several P/Women suspected of being lesbians.

Supt. Murphy phoned re lesbian inquiry … Saw Messrs C. Chant and T. Mahon re lesbian P/Women approaching Union, and some of their allegations.

Saw Supt. Murphy re … and lesbian P/women.

Saw Supt. Murphy re reports on lesbian p/women.

With p/w … discussed duties, … and lesbian p/women until 7 pm.[145]

From November 1978 until October 1980 Lewis personally interviewed female applicants, apparently with a view to keeping out lesbians. His diaries indicate that he interviewed at least 91 women. One woman recalls:

We were interviewed by a panel and then we got called back again to be interviewed by the Commissioner, who at that time was Mr Lewis. He would just call you in and talk to you about why you wanted to join. It was just a very general chat for five or 10 minutes or so.

With what sort of questions?

It was 14 years ago now, although I remember when he asked me about why I wanted to join I talked about doing Juvenile Aid.. That was probably the right thing to do at the time when I wasn't aware of it. I was extremely nervous anyway... I found out later that men didn't go through that process, just the women.[146]

During the Lewis years there was no formal policy of discriminatory deployment other than the exclusion of women — 'for safety reasons'

— from the Public Safety Response Team and from small isolated stations. Women served in the CIB, Traffic Branch, Prosecutions, Training and Mobile Patrols but were typically not found in small elite squads such as Water Police, Stock Squad and Air Wing.[147] Nonetheless, there was a strong feeling amongst that there was a de facto policy of keeping women to traditional areas such as juvenile aid, sexual offences, and in secretarial and clerical functions: 'You had to fight your way out of the office'.[148] In the late-1970s there were renewed complaints from policeman's wives about women in patrol cars and in some areas policewomen were taken off night time mobile patrols.[149]

In Queensland, for most of the 1980s, applications were not accepted from married women or women with children. Women in the force who married were allowed to continue in employment but it appears that Commissioner Lewis exercised his discretion under legislation to veto married applicants.[150] Furthermore, it was claimed that selection criteria for both males and females were biased against divorcees and people separated or in de facto relationships. An entry in Lewis's diary made very soon after he became commissioner refers to a 'Conference with top officers re policy on P/Women living in de facto relationships'.[151] No indication is given of the content of the discussions but it probably involved opposition to such relationships. One officer recalled:

> You couldn't tell anyone that you were in a de facto relationship. I had met someone after I got into the job and we were living in a de facto relationship for a while and it was very hush hush.
> *What would happen?*
> Oh you'd be transferred, separated.[152]

Following criticism in the media in mid-1987, applications were accepted by married women. However, the Past and Present Policewomen's Association claimed that biased selection criteria were still employed.[153]

Discrimination also manifested itself in neglect and in a broad discretion left to supervisors to treat women according to the supervisor's own prejudices. The following description of conditions in the Rape Squad in this period demonstrates the kind of ghetto environment many women worked in:

> When I was working in the Rape Squad we weren't very well looked after and we worked under atrocious conditions but we were necessary and

we were an all female squad so in that sense we were fairly unique. We didn't have any office or anything like that. We'd interview, we'd talk to rape victims in amongst this huge information bureau system. Phones are ringing and things like that. We had to work on our own. If we were seen talking to each other [as part of the counselling process, talking on the job, we were seen not to be working. So therefore they would give us jobs answering the phones and doing motor vehicle checks and things like that. We had quite a few women that left and went out on stress recovering in a psychiatric ward for a couple of weeks just for a break — had a break down. But I didn't realise at that time it was a fairly tough area. Women wouldn't go into it because of the reasons I just outlined so it was difficult to get out as well. I was there for three years on a temporary transfer.[154]

In fact, squad members were expected to do little more than conduct interviews and provide victim support. Investigations and prosecutions were handed over to male detectives.[155]

The discretion exercised by officers in charge had a crucial impact on women's opportunities. In most cases it seems that administrative latitude was exercised against women. One woman, for example, made repeated attempts to join the Dog Squad. Some members of the squad made a positive response to her enquiries but when she spoke to the officer in charge he said that only married officers could have dogs. (Dogs were kept at home by their handlers.) The woman knew that at least one officer in the squad was not married. Then she was told that women did not have the strength to manage dogs, although the woman had no problem managing her two Irish wolf hounds. She was then told that owning dogs precluded her from keeping a police dog. When a vacancy occurred she was told that she had to own a house.[156] Many men continued to avoid being rostered with women and in this received support from supervisors.[157] At least one woman felt that she was assigned duties in the hope that she would buckle under pressure:

> When in '78 I was unceremoniously dumped into Traffic Branch, people were hopeful that one of two things would happen. One: I'd hate 'real' police work because, after all, I was a Whitrod office dolly and it would all be too much for me and I'd courteously resign. Or, if they were real lucky, I'd get run over intercepting someone on traffic.[158]

For some, sexual harassment was a major obstacle to be negotiated as part of an intimidating and stressful experience as a probationary constable:

Harassment didn't really come till later on for me, like: 'Oh well, if you are not interested you must be gay' ... all that sort of stuff. But X ... got stationed at city station. City station was known for police that couldn't be put anywhere else: the drunks and alcoholics. I remember her telling me in her first 12 months she was typing and one of the drunken sergeants was trying to kiss her on the neck and had pinned her under the table, pushed the chair in. She couldn't escape and she called out to the senior sergeant for assistance. He said, 'Oh no, that is between you and such-and-such'. And I was outraged. I said, 'Why didn't you do something?' She said, 'What could I do. It was my first 12 months. They could sack me'.[159]

The Queensland Fitzgerald Inquiry

In Queensland, a major corruption inquiry in the late-1980s serendipitously led to major improvements for women in policing. Lewis was forced to stand down when the inquiry began work in 1987. The Fitzgerald report, tabled in 1989, associated high level police corruption with maladministration in both the police and government. In 1991 Lewis was sentenced to 14 years jail for participation in a protection racket. 219 individuals, including police, brothel keepers, SP bookmakers and a handful of politicians were charged with corruption related offences.[160]

In 1987, complaints had begun to come into Lewis and the police minister from politicians, women's groups, and middle level police management regarding shortages of policewomen.[161] Following Lewis's resignation, Acting Commissioner Redmond ordered a State-wide survey of the need for policewomen. Almost all the inspectors and superintendents who responded saw only the narrowest of roles for women and, according to the survey, an additional 45 police-women were required on top of the existing 272 in order to achieve an optimum level of approximately 6%. Redmond decided to aim for this figure by increasing intakes over a 2- to 3-year period.[162] By 1989 a policy had been adopted of increasing the proportion of women to 7% by recruiting 20% women in each intake.[163]

In 1989, the Past and Present Policewomen's Association — formed in 1981 to mark the 50th anniversary of the appointment of women police in Queensland — made a submission to the Fitzgerald Inquiry, focusing mainly on administrative issues. Christine Lidgard and Jill Bolen took the lead in developing the paper, which strongly recommended promotion by merit and the removal of discriminatory barriers in recruitment. The submission noted that research indicated a stronger service orientation on the part of women police and that this was in line with the more desirable philosophy of community policing. In the context of corruption allegations, it was also noted that women appeared to be much less susceptible to misconduct.[164]

The Policewomen's Association submission found an echo in the Fitzgerald Inquiry's report, handed down in 1989. In his comments on personnel issues, Fitzgerald made it clear that discrimination against women was part of the norm of insularity and cynicism that he identified in the force. He noted that 'an informal process has operated to keep the number of female police officers selected in any intake to between 5 and 12% although women comprise 25% of applicants'.[165] It was suggested that any assumption that training policewomen was a poor investment because of high dropout rates was no longer relevant. In the five years prior to 1989 a higher proportion of men resigned than women. Fitzgerald recommended that quotas be abandoned in favour of recruitment by merit and, like Whitrod, saw an increase in the number of women as part of positive cultural change within the police.[166]

A new Labor government swept into power on a reformist platform in 1989 as the National Party government fell into disarray. Fitzgerald's recommendations for appointment by merit were reflected in the new *Police Service Administration Act 1990*. The first female Acting Inspector had been appointed in 1989. Five policewomen quickly received promotions to Inspector level in 1990. In November 1989, the Acting Commissioner Training and Legal, referring specifically to the Fitzgerald recommendations, directed that there be no female quota in recruitment.[167] Figure 3.2 shows a dramatic increase in the number of female recruits around 1990. By 1993, Queensland was approaching the national average of 12.4% of women police. Women were 11.4% of sworn personal.[168] As Figure 3.2 shows, in the 1991/92 period, women made up 28.7% of applicants and 35.4% of recruits, well above the national average of 22% female recruits.[169] It is probable that female applicants were more highly qualified, given greater emphasis on educational criteria in selection. Commissioner Noel Newnham's main contribution appears to have been to stay out of things.

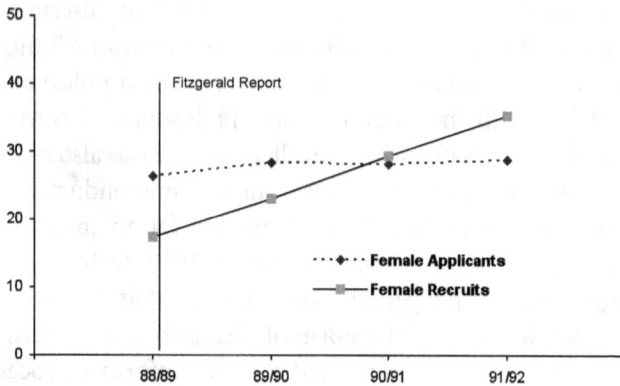

Figure 3.2
Percentages of female applicants and female recruits, QPS, 1988/89–1991/2[170]
Note: Progressive percentages. Female Applicants: 26.3, 28.3, 28.1, 28.7. Female
Recruits: 17.4, 23.1, 29.4, 35.4.

The Fitzgerald reforms created turmoil in the police in the first few
years of the 1990s and the influx of women appears to have been seen
as one more imposition on a police service that felt put upon by out-
siders. As in the early-1970s, the influx of women occasioned a generally hostile reaction. This time concerns centred around a new type of
officer: the short female:

> A lot of the reaction had to do with the fact that it wasn't just 'women'
> that were coming into the job but small women. Because at the same time
> that we had an increase in women the height and weight limit restrictions
> had been lifted. So in the previous year where you had to be 5'4" if you
> were a woman to get into the job, there was no longer any sort of restric-
> tion … It was those particular women that the senior officers and opera-
> tional officers objected to. They related it to working with a child,
> somebody who couldn't hold up their end of the deal in a brawl … You
> know, you have these real tiny women who were flat out seeing over a
> tablecloth.[171]

Conclusion

The period from the mid-1950s into the early-1990s saw enormous
advances for women police, especially in their assignment to general
duties and mixed patrols. Women police went mainstream with the
closures of the women police units, achievement of full powers and
equal pay across the country, adoption of uniforms and integration

into the rank structure. Nonetheless, the revolution was incomplete. The number of female officers crept up but remained at very low levels, reaching only 12% in the early-1990s. Discretionary forms of discrimination persisted, especially in recruitment and assignment. The period also saw some early applications of anti-discrimination legislation in policing. Sadly, time would show that police managers had to be forced by law to act in ways that were fair, if not scientific, in their approach to gender issues.

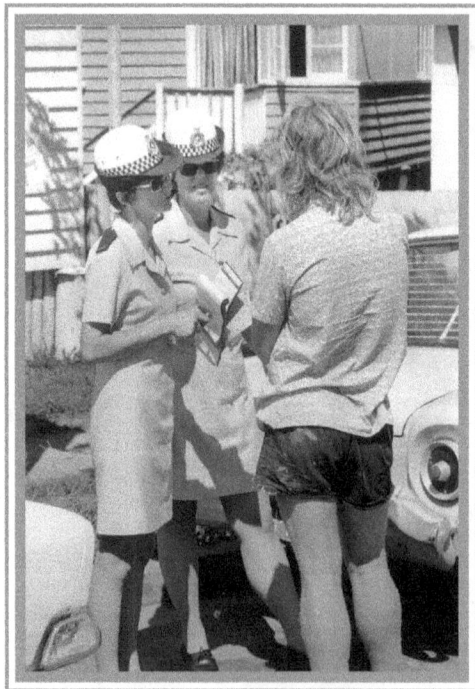

Queensland policewomen on the job circa 1973.

Chapter 4

Affirmative Action
and Divergent Practices

Over the period from the 1970s to the 1990s, Australian jurisdictions introduced general anti-discrimination legislation and equal
employment opportunity legislation targeting the public sector.
The new legislation had profound implications for women police
— although the benefits were often slow to flow down into police
personnel practices, and the moderate affirmative action orientation of the equal employment opportunity (EEO) legislation was
often avoided in substance. Nonetheless, developments in the
1990s set the stage for a consistent, if fairly passive, application
of equity principles across policing in the 2000s. Ninety years
after the appointment of the first women police, aspiring female
police officers and women in the job were largely protected by
law from the policy caprices of senior officers and from on-the-
job harassment and discrimination by colleagues and supervisors. There were also programs and policies in place to
encourage and support women. Part-time, later 'flexible',
employment was a stand-out example — with benefits for male
officers as well.

New Laws

The development of equity regulation in Australia involved a two-
stage process on a piecemeal jurisdictional basis from the 1970s.
Initially, legislation prohibiting sex discrimination — and other
forms of discrimination — was introduced that was common to all
sectors of society. This legislation was essentially passive because it
simply required non-discrimination. This meant that an occupation could be largely free of direct discrimination but have very
few women in total, and even fewer women in management or specialist positions, because of lack of applications from women.[1]
Hidden forms of discrimination through attitudes, inappropriate
practices and discretionary decision-making could also operate
against women.

In most cases, police simply ignored the legislation until external forces obliged a response. Christine Nixon describes how brave litigants forced the New South Wales Police to obey the law:[2]

> [In] 1980 … Victoria Carr, a rejected police applicant, took the Police Force to the Anti-Discrimination Board over a quota system which imposed strict limits on the numbers of women employed yearly by the Police Service. She was able to prove that the quota was discriminatory and the service was directed to abolish the quota system. As part of this settlement … From 1980 women were transferred directly to general duties after training and continued in this phase of duty unless they wished to apply for a transfer.
>
> In 1981 Eileen Thompsen brought an action against the Police Service claiming discrimination on the grounds of marital status. As a married woman, she had been denied entry to the Police Service. The Anti-Discrimination Board found in her favour and the barrier was lifted. Also in 1981, the Women Police Office was disbanded and the last Officer-in-Charge of Women Police retired in 1982.
>
> In 1982, women were integrated into the male seniority system. They were placed back into positions equal to those of the men with whom they had joined. What was not taken into account was that a small number of women had been denied promotion due to lack of vacancies in the women's seniority system and had suffered financial loss due to the situation.

As a result of the limits of anti-discrimination law, a second generation of legislation was introduced that required active measures to encourage equity. Deference to the private sector meant that this legislation was focused on government departments. Moderate affirmative action legislation, encouraging support for women, but without quotas, was applied progressively to all federal and states agencies. In the main, the innocuous term 'equal opportunity' was adopted in the title of Acts. However, the approach usually involved some 'affirmative action' in the sense that special measures (or a degree of preferential treatment) was expected in order to increase overall equality for women (and other target groups). This included a requirement to submit annual plans on strategies to encourage women, and to report and evaluate progress. Examples of possible strategies include targeted promotions, career planning workshops, women's advisory committees, workplace childcare, prizes and scholarships, reserved places on selection committees for women, and re-joining campaigns. Independent equity agencies were established to administer the legislation.

Queensland in the 1990s was very much a model of the new equity-oriented police service.[3] An EEO Joint Management/Union Consultative Committee was established in late-1991, an EEO Co-

Ordinator was appointed and an EEO Unit set up. Specific actions reported in 1994 included:

- the promotion of EEO principles in service journals, information sessions and an information kit
- the development of in-service Competency Acquisition Program modules, Equity and Sexual Harassment
- selection and training of Sexual Harassment Referral Officers
- sexual harassment awareness sessions
- the inclusion of an EEO component in the Executive Development Program
- the development of a non-discriminatory language guide and gradual removal of all discriminatory language from service documents
- the creation of part-time work (eight of 10 police who took up part-time work were women).[4]

Also in the mid- to late-1990s in Queensland, six weeks paid maternity leave was available; a free child care referral service was introduced, available to all members; a Women's Advisory Group was established; followed by a Career Planning Unit, Career Planning Officers and a state-wide mentoring program for women; a female officer was appointed to the Senior Executive Conference; and a policy was intro-duced of female representation on internal committees.[5]

By the 1990s, Australian jurisdictions had a fairly common set of equity laws that applied to police departments. A 2001 study of administering agencies with jurisdiction over police set out the legis-lation and the regulators in place at the end of the 1990s, going into the 2000s, as shown in Table 4.1[6]. Some jurisdictions had separate agencies. In others, equity was managed within a larger public service management commissions. Police responses to this new legislative regime, and the management of police performance by government regulatory agencies, were the subject of a series of studies by the author and colleagues published in 1995, 2000, 2004 and 2010.

The Late-1980s to the Early-1990s

The first national study on the status of women police focused on recruitment and training, was published in 1995, covering the five year period 1988 to 1993.[7] The data showed some yawning gaps between female application and recruitment rates. In Western Australia, from 1990 to 1993, women were 24.9% of applicants and

Table 4.1 Australian Equity Legislation and Regulatory Agencies 2001[6]

Location	Type	Legislation	Regulator
SA	AD AA	Sex Discrimination Act 1975 Equal Opportunity Act 1984	Office of the Commissioner for Equal Opportunity
NSW	AD	Anti-Discrimination Act 1977	Office of the Director of Equal
	AA AA?	Anti-Discrimination Act 1977 (amended 1980) State Service Act 2000* (not applicable to sworn officers)	Opportunity in Public Employment
NT	AD AA	Anti-Discrimination Act 1996 Public Sector Employment & Management Act 1998	Office of the Commissioner for Public Employment
C'wealth	AD AA	Sex Discrimination Act 1984 (not applicable to sworn officers) Affirmative Action Act 1986 (not applicable to sworn officers)	Minister for Justice
VIC	AD AA	Equal Opportunity Act 1984 (amended 1995) Public Authorities (Equal Employment Opportunity) Act 1990	Equal Opportunity Commission
WA	AD AA	Equal Opportunity Act 1984 Equal Opportunity Act 1984 (Part IX, EO in Public Employment)	Office of Equal Employment Opportunity
QLD	AD AA	Anti-Discrimination Act 1991 Equal Opportunity in Public Employment Act 1992	Office of the Public Service Commissioner
TAS	AD	Anti-Discrimination Act 1994	Office of the State Service Commissioner

Note: AD = anti-discrimination, AA = affirmative action.
* The Act is not explicitly an affirmative action Act but it authorises the Anti-Discrimination Commissioner to give directives. A 2002 Directive, 'Workplace Diversity', included requirements for active measures to encourage the public employment of under-represented groups, and includes standard requirements of planning and monitoring.

16.3% of recruits and cadets (re-joiners). In Victoria, between 1987 and 1990, after which recruitment was suspended, women were 27.7% of applicants and 19.5% of recruits. Obstacle course tests remained the main cause of the attrition of female applicants. For example, a 1990 police report *The Impact of Equal Opportunity on Policing in Victoria*, showed that, in 1989, 33.0% of women passed on initial testing compared to 88.9% of males.[8] Of the 51% of women who repeated the test at a later stage, 29% passed. Women also performed at a lower level in interviews: 75.9% of women passed compared to 80.6% of men.

Some other jurisdictions where data were available showed less dramatic differences in female application and recruitment rates: -2.6% in South Australia, -3.7% in Tasmania, and -2.1% in Queensland. However, there was significant change in Queensland over this period. Between 1988/89 and 1989/90, women were 27.3% of applicants and 20.9% of recruits. Between 1990/91 and 1991/92, women were 28.4% of applicants and 31.5% of recruits. As detailed in the previous chapter, the improvement in Queensland related to removal of quotas and improvements in educational criteria. A similar level of change was evident in New South Wales. In the period 1989 to 1993, women were 24.4% of applicants and 20.2% of recruits. However, from 1989 to 1990 women were 23.7% of applicants and 16.2% of recruits; while from 1991 to 1993 women were 25.1% of applicants and 30.3% of recruits. The change coincided with the phasing in of a moderate preferential selection system.

Two jurisdictions showed better results for women in recruitment over the full periods of available data. In the Northern Territory, in the absence of a physical fitness test, the difference between application and selection rates for women was +0.3%. A spokesperson suggested women performed better in interviews. Australian Federal Police (AFP) recruitment processes favoured women by +3.5%. The AFP also had no pre-entry physical fitness tests, and a spokesperson attributed the higher recruitment rate to the fact female applicants had higher qualifications and performed better in interviews and written examinations.

In academy training there were also differences in attrition rates. In Victoria, there attrition rate was 11.0% for males and 13.4% for females. No data were available from Western Australia. In South Australia the rates were 7.2% for men and 4% for women. Tasmania had a 6.4% drop out rate for men and 0% for women. In Queensland, the male rate was 1.5% and the female rate was 15.2% — but with an improvement in female graduation rates from 1990. In 1991/92, women were 35.4% of recruits and 31.6% of Academy graduates. In the Federal Police, women were 27.8% of recruits and 27.9% of graduates. In New South Wales, the attrition rate for males was 14.0% and 6.4% for females. In the Northern Territory, 16.9% of males and 27.9% of females failed to complete training — although the numbers of recruits were very small.

The 1993 study was focused on recruitment, but some data on separations were also included. The limited data indicated women were leaving at about the same rate as men but more women were resigning compared to the bulk of males who separated via retirement. Very limited data were available on complaints of harassment and discrimination. The most detailed data were from South Australia:

> From 1989 to 1993 there were 47 complaints of sex discrimination. All complaints were by women. Twenty-one concerned sexual harassment; seven, duties; six, pregnancy; one, facilities; ten, rostering; and two, transfer/promotion. Most complainants (63.8%) did not desire action. Other complaints were resolved by informal conciliation (8.5%), disciplinary action (6.3%), 'action taken' (10.6%) and EO Commission inquiry (10.6%).

The 1990 Victorian Police report cited above was one of the few revealing publicly available reports on EEO in policing at the time. A survey indicated that 19.2% of women officers in Victoria, compared to 7% of men, had experienced gender related discrimination. One interesting finding was that 40.3% of sub-officers said they had rostered female officers onto duties considered less dangerous. There was also very little evidence of awareness of EEO principles. At the same time, the survey found that the very large majority of respondents believed the sexes were getting on well and that women were as capable as men in performing general duties. Nonetheless, approximately 80% of male officers believed men were better at handling violent situations and they felt more confident with a male partner. Women's attitudes were fairly similar, with approximately two-thirds expressing less confidence in women's capabilities during physical confrontation.

The Victoria report also included survey data on perceived discrimination: 17.7% of female officers and 2.8% of males said they had been deterred from applying for specialist positions, most notably CIB and Dog Squad. In relation to sexual harassment, 63.1% of women, compared to 14.2% of men, said they had experienced sexual harassment. Very few persons experiencing harassment made a formal complaint, with concerns about repercussions cited as the main reason. Approximately three-quarters of complaints were dealt with through counselling of the parties or forms of intervention by supervisors. A small number of grievances reached the EEO Coordinator.

The Mid- to Late-1990s

The second national study,[9] published in 2000, was focused on the period 1994 to 1998, and included more detail on rank and the quality of EEO data. Figure 4.1 shows the percentages of female officers and recruits over the period of the study. The results were similar to the 1993 study in showing a steady but slight increase in the proportion of female officers of approximately 0.4% per annum — up from 13.7% in 1994 to 15.2% in 1998. The upward trajectory in sworn officers was driven by the flow through of female recruits — up from 27.5% in 1996 to 36.2% in 1998.

Table 4.2 reports the data represented in Figure 4.1, separated out by jurisdiction. The table shows considerable inconsistency between agencies. Western Australia still had a very poor recruitment rate of 12.1% females in 1998 (following a surge from 14.4% in 1996 to 25.6% in 1997). Victoria stood out as unique in having a reduction in number of female officers — from 13.4% in 1997 to 13.3% in 1998. At the same time, the number of recruits in Victoria in 1998 was in the middle range at 29.3%. In the Northern Territory, the percentage

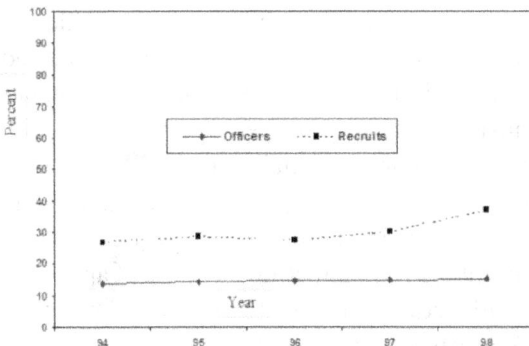

Figure 4.1
Female Officers and Recruits, Australia, 1994–1998.

Table 4.2 Percentages of female police and recruits by agency, Australia, 1994–1998

	1994		1995		1996		1997		1998	
	O	R	O	R	O	R	O	R	O	R
AFP	16.7	34.6	17.2	42.1	18.6	20.0	18.7	50.0	19.1	30.0
Tas.	11.8	31.2	12.5	40.7	14.8	30.0	15.1	26.3	16.0	28.3
NSW	12.2	26.6	13.1	32.3	14.0	36.4	15.5	34.6	16.8	42.6
WA	9.5	18.6	9.5	7.9	9.8	14.4	11.0	25.6	11.3	12.1
NT	19.4	22.0	19.5	21.5	15.8	—	15.9	20.8	17.7	17.1
Vic.	13.4	19.0	13.8	23.6	13.8	19.2	13.4	25.2	13.3	29.3
SA	14.6	37.7	14.7	36.3	17.2	44.4	15.4	34.6	16.6	36.0
Qld	12.2	25.4	12.6	25.6	13.3	28.3	14.1	26.1	15.1	34.8
Total	13.7	26.9	14.1	28.7	14.6	27.5	14.8	30.4	15.2	36.2

Note: O = officer; R = recruit

of female officers fell from 19.4% female officers in 1994 to 15.8% in 1996, and then rose to 17.7% in 1998. The problem, however, with the Northern Territory data was that Aboriginal Community Police Officers (ACPOs) and auxiliary officers were included in the count. These officers are not fully sworn. New South Wales, South Australia and Queensland had relatively high rates of female recruitment at 42.6%, 36.0% and 34.8% respectively in 1998.

The findings showed a fairly consistent pattern in outcomes, with three main types of departments: 'high achievers', 'moderate achievers' and 'laggards'. New South Wales and Queensland stood out as high achievers, with recruitment of women up to 33% and above, and affirmative action support programs in place. Tasmania, South Australia, the Northern Territory and the AFP showed moderate achievement. Victoria and Western Australia were notable for lack of progress in advancing women police.

The study was not able to obtain any useful data on deployment. Some useful data on other measures were obtained from a few departments. In South Australia, the data showed that women were recruited in numbers approximating their rate of application. Data on applications and recruitment from Queensland showed contradictory tendencies. Women who applied through the normal recruitment process were recruited at a slightly higher rate than applied. At the same time, an alternative 'rejoiner' entry program, introduced in 1994 to reduce training costs and the large number of trainee constables at the front line, had the effect of reducing the total proportion of female recruits. Queensland also introduced an obstacle course test in recruitment in 1994 (detailed later) and was then forced to modify it because it lacked validity and impacted negatively on women. South Australia and Queensland also provided data on recruits and academy graduates, indicating no apparent problems with attrition of women from academy training.

In this period, New South Wales introduced a new training system whereby potential officers completed a university-based course at the academy and then applied for a job as a constable. It appeared that the tertiary study requirement, together with a marketing campaign focused on women, produced the best result in the study, with women making up 42.6% of beginning constables in 1998. This could be compared a female rate of application to the tertiary training program of 42.3%. However, the lack of data from the majority of jurisdictions mad it difficult to assess gender equity in recruitment across the jurisdictions.

Data on separations were supplied by the Northern Territory, Western Australia, Queensland and New South Wales. Again, the numbers indicated that female officers were separating at a rate approximating that of male officers. In the Northern Territory, from 1994 to 1998, women averaged 17.6% of officers and 17.9% of separations. In Western Australia, the figures were 10.2% and 10.9%; in Queensland, 13.4% and 14.4%; and New South Wales, 14.3% and 12.8%. However, a breakdown of the numbers showed that male separations were concentrated in retirements, whereas women were resigning before retirement age. In the Northern Territory, men were 100% of retirees; women were 20.7% of resignations but 17.6% of officers. In Western Australia, men were 98.8% of retirees; women were 15.3% of resignations but 10.2% of officers. In Queensland, men were 89.9% of retirees; women were 18.6% of resignations but 13.4% of officers. The best data, from New South Wales, showed that 'family/domestic' was a major category in the female resignation rate where reasons were listed. Women also predominated in the large category of resignations for unspecified reasons.

The study also obtained data on complaints of discrimination and harassment from New South Wales and Queensland. In New South

Wales, for the period 1991–97, there was a small number of complaints of 'harassment/discrimination', averaging 45 each year, with women making up 90% of complainants. Complaints from women were resolved 'formally' in 36% of cases and 'informally' in 64% of cases. Queensland showed a somewhat similar profile.

None of the departments was able to provide the number of male and female applications for promotion and the numbers promoted. However, the researchers were able to combine rank data and compare these over time. Figure 4.2 shows the proportion of women at different ranks across Australia in 1993 and 1998. The chart shows women were moving up the ranks, although at a very slow rate. For example, at Sergeant and above the average increase was 1.2%.

Table 4.3 shows these data broken down by department. Victoria, Western Australia and Tasmania showed minimal changes. There were

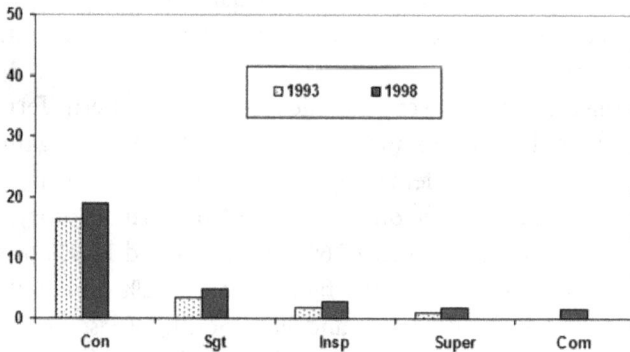

Figure 4.2
Percentage of females officers by rank, Australia, 1993 and 1998.

no increases in the number of women at Superintendent and above, and there were increases of approximately 1% at the ranks of Sergeant and Inspector. New South Wales was ahead overall, including the promotion of a few women into the very top Commissioner category.

Police departments in the middle group of moderate achievers were generally good performers in recruitment and training — recruiting and graduating about the same number of women as applied — but this was representative of a largely passive approach to equity management with very limited affirmative action for most of

Table 4.3 Change in percentage of women by rank, all jurisdictions, 1993 and 1998

Rank	AFP	TAS	NSW	WA	NT	VIC	SA	QLD	Total
Commissioners	0.0	0.0	+25.0	0.0	0.0	0.0	0.0	0.0	+1.7
Superintendents	+6.3	0.0	-1.1	0.0	+7.6	0.0	+2.6	+2.3	+0.8
Inspectors	+1.2	+2.1	+1.7	+1.0	-0.4	0.0	-2.0	+1.3	+1.0
Sergeants	0.0	+0.4	+2.7	+1.2	+2.7	+1.6	+0.2	+0.9	+1.5
Constables	+2.9	+1.1	+5.3	+1.7	+3.9	-1.8	+2.2	+4.5	+2.6
Average	+3.4	+1.2	+6.7	+1.3	+3.5	-0.2	+0.75	+2.25	+1.52

the '90s. The two departments in third group — the laggards — clearly discriminated in recruitment, especially through the use of difficult obstacle course tests. This flowed through to low percentages of female officers.

The big picture was discouraging. Nationally, women made up only 15% of police, with very small improvements in numbers each year, very low promotion rates, and very few women — 2% — in senior management. While the high achievers — New South Wales and Queensland — showed promise, across the country there was also an indicative problem of higher female attrition, lack of family friendly policies, and signs of ongoing problems of sexual harassment and discrimination.

The study also found that police departments were not collecting the data they needed to properly assess their performance across all aspects of gender equity. The researchers concluded that:[14]

> Interventions to address problems cannot be developed without proper diagnostic research. For example, we could ask the question: Are women still concentrated in more traditional areas of female employment (such as juvenile aid and child abuse) and excluded from specialist squads and detective work? At present, no agency appears to be able to answer this question.

No agency obtained a perfect score for data quality, although New South Wales and Queensland stood out with scores of 10/14 and 7/14 respectively. The remaining departments received scores of two or less. In some cases, such as Victoria, this could be related to very poor equity management plans. However, in other cases, most notably Tasmania, quality equity management plans failed to generate quality data. Also of note was the poor performance of the AFP. This was considered 'surprising, given its reputation for innovation in modern management principles such as the use of performance indicators'.[15]

Overall, the results demonstrated 'a preponderance of the symbolic purposes of law (such as creating the appearance of a just regime) over instrumentalist purposes (such as real equality).'[16] The study: [17]

> supports the observations of police scholars that police are adept at evading genuine accountability and of maintaining their operational independence ... The problem is exacerbated by the passivity, not just of governments, but of regulatory bodies such as EEO agencies.

More specifically, the study found that the attitude of police commissioners was a key explanatory factor in performance in equity. In backwards Western Australia, Brian Bull was in charge from 1985 to 1994, followed by Robert Falconer from 1994 to 1999. In Victoria, from 1993 to 2001, Chief Commissioner Neil Comrie presided over a regime notorious for its misogyny.

Brute Force

During Comrie's tenure, the Federation of Community Legal Centres Victoria produced two reports in 1993 and 1999. The first report, *Brute Force: The Need for Affirmative Action in the Victorian Police Force*, critiqued the 1990 Victoria Police report cited earlier, *The Impact of Equal Opportunity on Policing in Victoria*, obtained under Freedom of information. Brute Force highlighted the very low representation of women in the Victoria Police in 1992 (14.4%), the even lower rates at senior ranks (1.8% at Inspector or above) and in country postings (< 10%). The report also highlighted the concentration of women in administrative and welfare duties and their underrepresentation in detective work and other more elite areas, including in the Special Operations Group (known as 'the Sons of God'). The report also highlighted the worsening discrimination resulting from the introduction of a physical agility test:[18]

> The major reason so few women are recruited is that they fail to pass a physical agility test. A new agility test was introduced in January 1989. The report states that since the introduction of this test the female pass rate dropped 24% from 57% in 1988 to 33% in 1989, while the male pass rate remained at 88%. The report does not provide any explanation as to why the test was introduced. The agility test discriminates against women in a number of ways.

The agility test includes a fat test. The current body fat measures allow males 21% body fat and females 24% body fat. The body fat rates for an average male is 18% and a female is 28%. Women naturally have greater than 10% more body fat than men. Women have more fat cells than men, and the cells are larger. The test requires that females must have four per cent less body fat than the average female while males who pass are allowed three per cent more body fat than the average male. In other words women need to be leaner than average to pass the force's fat test while men can be flabbier than average and still pass. However, the report erroneously states that the allowable body fat ratios accurately represent the physiological differences between men and women. The fat test requirement is clearly discrimination within the definition of discrimination in the *Equal Opportunity Act (Vic.) 1984* in that it is more difficult for females to pass such a test than males and it is not a reasonable test.

In addition the agility test has a pronounced emphasis on upper body strength. Just over two-thirds of female applicants fail the part of the agility test which requires great upper body strength. Only 11% of male applicants fail these tests.

Women, relative to men have more strength in their lower body than upper body. Women's leg strength is significantly closer to men's than is their arm strength. Whilst a test that looked at overall strength would fail more women than men, because on average men are stronger than women, a test which primarily tests upper body strength will fail significantly more women than men.

The report comments that applicants who fail the test can go away and build themselves up and apply for the test again. This does not address the question of discrimination but amounts to advising those people who fail, mainly women, to go away and work to make themselves more like men. The agility test, like the fat test, discriminates unlawfully against women.

The Brute Force report also highlighted a higher fail rate for female applicants in the interviews.

The Victoria Police report included a survey which found that 44% of female recruits alleged they had been subject to 'sexist language, disparaging comments, questions of marital status and comments on female ineffectiveness or their physical limitations, despite the fact that these women had already passed the agility test.'[19] The Brute Force report went on to link the male dominated and misogynistic culture in the Victoria police with an inadequate response to domestic violence and rape, and inappropriate treatment of women in police custody.

The second report, *Brute Force II: The Continuing Need for Affirmative Action in the Victorian Police Force*, published in 1999, demonstrated the abject failure of police leaders to make improvements.[20] It included four case studies of personal experiences of discrimination and harassment, including detail on the successful and high-profile Narell McKenna case before the state's Anti-Discrimination Tribunal outlined later.

The Premier State

In New South Wales, Christine Nixon became Assistant Commissioner Personnel with support from the progressive Commissioner John Avery. In this role she was able to introduce a number of reforms that benefitted women. Some of these were described in a 2003 interview:[21]

> *So you were the one who got rid of the obstacle course test in NSW?*
>
> Yes. I was in charge of that area so it was easy! It was around '95–'96. The other issue was how you attracted more women. I came to visit Victoria in 1992, and Victoria had twice as many women apply to become police officers as NSW had. So I went back to NSW and said we could do a lot more advertising to attract women. So we started a recruitment campaign, especially in schools. Of course, in Victoria what was happening was that women who came in didn't progress. They just left. But in NSW we had a lot of different support programs that allowed them to come together to develop leadership capacities. Getting good selection panels that didn't hold women back was important. Celebrating the 85th anniversary of women in policing [1995] was a wonderful event and drew attention to the issue. Having a thousand women march through the streets of Sydney was staggering. I got accused a lot of using the system to support women, but I didn't worry too much about that.

Nixon was replaced as head of personnel by a civilian David Gill. According to Gill, residual discriminatory effects of physical tests motivated him to introduce a system of limited preferential selection of female candidates.[22] Small numbers of males at the bottom of the recruitment lists were replaced with recommended females candidates. The males were given places in the following round. This targeted recruitment of women saw female recruit numbers gradually increase from 17% in 1989 to 33% in 1993, above the application rate of 29%.[23]

But the positive numbers behind the 'high achiever' label for New South Wales hid a dark reality. Women were coming into the force in large numbers, where they were exposed to bigots, perverts and sex pests. In the mid-1990s, Jeanna Sutton carried out a study of women police across the state, with 822 questionnaires returned.[24] There were some positive findings. For example, 91% of survey respondents thought policing was a secure occupation. Views on the application of promotion by merit were mixed, although

66% felt women had equal access to promotion opportunities. At the same time, 83% believed sexist attitudes and behaviours were entrenched in the Service, and 75% believed women needed to become 'one of the boys' to obtain acceptance. The results regarding sexual harassment were deeply troubling:

- 80% of female officers said they had experienced 'uninvited teasing, jokes, remarks or questions of a sexual nature ... once, 2–5 times or more, with 43% of women reporting more than 10 times'.
- 48% had experienced 'uninvited pressure for dates ... 7% of officers experienced this pressure on more than 10 occasions'.
- 35% reported 'uninvited pressure for sexual favours ... at least once or more with 6% of officers reporting more than 10 times'.
- 60% reported 'uninvited sexually suggestive looks or gestures once, 2–5 times or more with 21% of women reporting more than 10 times'.
- 56% experienced 'uninvited and deliberate touching, stroking or pinching ... at least once, 2–5 times or more with 12% of respondents reporting more than 10 times.'[25]

Despite these chronic levels of abuse, 'the majority (70%) reported that they would not feel comfortable (in general) approaching the EEO Unit, their Patrol Commander (69%) or their immediate supervisor (58%)'.[26]

The NPRU and ACPR Reports

Discussions at the First Australasian Women Police Conference in 1996 led to the National Police Research Unit (NPRU) initiating a study of problems and issues facing women in policing.[27] An 'experiences in the workplace' survey was developed and distributed to sworn and unsworn male and female employees up to the rank of Senior Sergeant in five police departments in 1998/1999. The findings from the 1,859 returned questionnaires were published in the report *Contemporary Issues Facing Women in Policing in 2002*.[28] The results indicated numerous common experiences, highlighting the commitment of all staff to their work and the stressful nature of policing for sworn officers. Apart from the stresses of working with offenders and victims of crime, issues of child care, moving home for work, long hours, and being called out figured prominently as problems for both male and female officers. At the same time, these stressors were stronger for single parents and for both sworn and unsworn women.

The study also found that female police officers were less likely than the other three groups to want to be promoted, but they were also more likely than male police officers to remain in their present employment. Males generally showed greater confidence than females in their ability to do their work and get promoted. In addition:[29]

> Women (both sworn and nonsworn) rated several career barriers more highly than did (sworn and nonsworn) men, namely: lack of adequate childcare; lack of personal confidence; prejudice of colleagues; social pressures; Men's Club network; and sexual discrimination. On the other hand, men (both sworn and nonsworn) rated lack of career guidance, attitudes of senior staff and racial discrimination more highly than did women.

No direct questions were asked about sexual harassment. However, sworn and unsworn women were also more likely to state they had experienced the following:[30]

- being subjected to threatening or abusive language
- being humiliated in front of fellow workers/members of the public
- having undesirable rumours spread about them
- being victimised because of a reasonable refusal to undertake tasks.

One of the issues highlighted at the Second Australasian Conference of Women and Policing, in 1999, was the paucity of women in senior management. This prompted a second study by the Australasian Centre for Policing Research (ACPR, which replaced the NPRU) — *Women in Senior Police Management* — published in 2001.[31] The centre surveyed police managers, including unsworn staff of the rank of Inspector and above or equivalent, in New Zealand and seven Australian departments, with 127 useable questionnaires. At the time, women made up only 3.6% of sworn officers at that level. The survey showed that sworn female officers reported having experienced much higher rates of discrimination at lower ranks (82%) than female unsworn staff (47%), male sworn officers (28%) and male unsworn staff (27%).[32] In their current position, 50% of female sworn officers said they had experienced discrimination compared to 45% of unsworn females, 36% of male unsworn staff and 20% of male sworn officers.[33] The main differences between male and female responses in the study were summarised as follows:[34]

> Women indicated that they found sexual discrimination, men's club, inflexible working patterns, lack of career guidance, prejudice of colleagues, social pressures and lack of confidence to be greater career barriers than did men. Women in the study also found that work spilled

over into their family life to a greater extent than did male respondents. Analysis of the qualitative information indicated that this was due to the belief that a good manager is willing to work long hours and be available after hours. Consequently, there was a perception that women with family responsibilities do not take the job seriously, and therefore they are under increased pressure to prove their worthiness as managers. It is these cultural expectations of police managers that appear to discourage women (or men with families) from making use of flexible policies.

The Regulators

What was unclear from available research from the 1990s was the extent to which equity agencies influenced police equity practices. A 2001 study was designed to address this deficit by examining how the regulatory agencies charged with facilitating and enforcing compliance with the legislation interacted with police departments.[35] The study entailed a written questionnaire sent to all the equity agencies listed at Table 4.1. A combination of begging and veiled threats of exposure — as uncooperative and secretive — eventually produced a 100% response rate. One might imagine these agencies to be staffed by very assertive feminist lawyers with an agenda to take on traditionally misogynist organisations, enforce the new regime of equity and help the sisters in uniform. The study results found the exact opposite. All the agencies were adequately legally empowered. Only one complained of insufficient resources. But they were all miserably passive. They simply rubber-stamped police reports, failed to demand proper data, failed to impose remedial plans on recalcitrant agencies, and failed to name and shame. The presence or absence of affirmative action legislation appeared important, but legal efficacy occurred primarily when police management adopted a cooperative approach or when civil cases stimulated change.

For example, there was an overwhelming body of international case law and scientific evidence to show that the notorious obstacle course tests used by the Western Australian and Victoria Police were invalid as selection tools.[36] But the regulators simply ignored the tests and the evidence. The upshot of this culture of under-regulation was that victims of discrimination and harassment were forced to take their complaints to the courts — a very hazardous and stressful course of action. The high profile Narell McKenna case illustrated the problem. The Brute Force II report summarised her case as follows:[37]

Narell McKenna

Senior Constable Narell McKenna took the Victoria Police to the Anti-Discrimination Tribunal because she no longer wanted to tolerate sexist attitudes, discrimination and harassment.

Ms McKenna endured endless demeaning and cruel derogatory comments from her male co-workers when she was stationed at the Bairnsdale police station. Not only was she subjected to constant sexist jokes about a woman's rightful place [in] the home, bedroom and kitchen, she was intrusively fondled, asked for oral sex and dragged kicking and screaming to a police cell. Enduring this type of abuse for two years led Ms McKenna to attempt suicide in 1997 and she still suffers from panic and anxiety attacks.

In trying to gain career advancement Ms McKenna again encountered discrimination. Ms McKenna applied for a four-wheel drive course, even after her fellow co-workers had stated, 'don't bother you won't get on it'. She was unsuccessful. When [she] asked why she was refused Ms McKenna was told it was because she 'was a girl' and it was a 'traditionally male position'.

Ms McKenna was also denied access to a number of other special duties. Completion of these special duties is important for career advancement because it proves the officer is responsible and can handle matters. Ms McKenna stated that 'she was not given an opportunity to do this work whereas male members of equal or lower rank were'. When Mr Heesom [her former supervisor] was questioned about restricting Ms McKenna's promotional opportunities, by denying access to special duties, he stated that 'I still don't think that there would be one station that would have a female in charge. I don't know that they are quite ready for that yet'.

The behaviour that Narell McKenna was forced to endure was so outrageous she was awarded an unprecedented amount of $125,000 by the Anti-Discrimination Tribunal.

Disappointingly, rather than accept the finding and work for positive change, Victoria Police chose to appeal this finding. The Supreme Court denied the appeal.

In 1998, after winning in the initial hearing, McKenna declared she had lost five years of her life.[38] However, it was to be another year before the unconscionable appeal by the Victoria government was defeated. McKenna also lost a large proportion of the damages payment to legal bills, and in 2000 she was still reportedly seeking full payment from the Victoria Police.[39]

Police avoidance of legal responsibilities was not confined to gender issues. In Queensland, in 1994, the Anti-Discrimination Tribunal ordered the Police Service to employ an applicant who was rejected because he wore contact lenses. The Tribunal rejected the service's claim that the physical requirements of policing precluded wearing contact lenses.[40]

Also in Queensland in 1994, the introduction of a bogus obstacle course test, based on pseudo-science, was endorsed by the equity agency, only to be removed at a much later date following an assessment by that state's anti-corruption body.[41] The test was introduced in response to police Union alarmism. In 1993, Union President John O'Gorman called for the re-introduction of height and weight restrictions following attacks on police officers. In *The Courier-Mail*, O'Gorman claimed that officers were concerned for their safety when working with 'smaller officers, especially women', who were an 'easy target for aggressive louts'.[42] O'Gorman conceded he could not cite any specific cases, and Commissioner O'Sullivan came out in support of women, stating that the service would remain an equal opportunity employer. He also expressed support for small policewomen: 'We have some very small policewomen but, let me tell you, they have plenty of fight in them'.[43]

Following the Fitzgerald reforms in Queensland and the introduction of equity legislation, the only physical tests in recruitment were a run, a medical check and a fire arms handling test. Following O'Gorman's claims, and despite O'Sullivan's comments, Assistant Commissioner Personnel and Training Greg Early authorised the introduction of the obstacle course test in recruitment. The test was devised by Academy physical skills staff, based on United States (US) models, which were based on US military post-recruitment training. The test supposedly represented a backyard chase scenario common in operational policing. The result was that for the first time in several years a higher proportion of males was recruited than females. In the first intake following the introduction of the test, the female application rate was 30.4%, while the recruit rate was 28.0%.[44]

In 1994, David Gill was appointed to the new civilian position of Director of Personnel. As noted above, Gill had introduced targeted recruitment of women in New South Wales. When he became aware of the impact of the physical competency test he brought in the preferential selection system while the test was under review. This helped moderate the negative effect of the test on female applicants.[45]

Catching up: Tasmania and the AFP

The moderate achieving police departments described above began to show signs of a more dynamic approach to gender equity from around 1995 as modernising commissioners responded positively to more active EEO whole of government agendas. In Tasmania, for example, police annual reports periodically included motherhood statements about equity. The 1996/97 annual report had a different tone: listing a set of 'major achievements' in equity. Among others, these were:[46]

- the training of 150 officers on EEO issues
- the implementation of a confidential Help Line to provide advice or information
- the production and distribution statewide of EEO posters entitled 'A Fair Go — EEO', which advertises the Help Line number
- satisfactory resolution of eleven EEO related complaints.

Subsequently, *The Saturday Mercury* picked up on equity initiatives when reporting on a Budget Estimates Committee hearing on the police department. Commissioner McCriedie, appointed in 1996, told the Committee that, 'the establishment of a police equal employment opportunity plan had created a framework for an increase in the number of women in the force, up from 166 in 1996–97 to 183 in 1997–98'.[47] At the same time, the newspaper noted that there was little progress at the top, with only one woman at the rank of Inspector despite the government's equity policy:

> Police Minister David Llewellyn conceded there was no plan to ensure that 35% of senior positions were filled by women by 2001 — the target set by the State Government for the senior executive service.[48]

In 2000, the *Hobart Mercury* reported on an extraordinary event: an academy class that was 45% female.[49] In 2001, Commissioner McCreadie stated in a newspaper report that

> Women have the capacity to do anything their male counterparts can do. More flexible workplace arrangements mean women with family commitments are now able to join and continue in their careers. We've broken down the impediments to age and family responsibilities.[50]

At the AFP, Commissioner Mick Palmer, appointed in 1994, was an outspoken supporter of women. In 1995, Palmer engaged Carmel Niland to review the force's performance in EEO. Niland's report, based on focus groups, was a classic study in the gap between formal organisational values and informal cultural practices.[51] Niland found that policewomen were resented by their male colleagues; their child-care responsibilities were seen as handicap that placed a burden on others; and they were passed over from promotion, or discouraged from applying, because of perceived deficiencies based on feminine characteristics.

In regard to sexual harassment, Niland made the following comments:[52]

> There are many elements of organisational cultures which make the implementation of real equality of opportunity difficult, if not impossible, despite the fact that the organisation has adopted EEO as a management practice and a goal, and this was the case with the AFP. The AFP had a strong anti-sexual harassment policy, a grievance system and some harassment contact officers, but it still had some serious cases of sexual harassment last year. Why?
>
> Let me give you an example. Five male police officers sexually harassed ten female police officers. The incidents included constant obscenities, touching, pushing, leering and spitting. The male superintendent observed the behaviour and did nothing. The women eventually complained to EEO. Some were ostracised and others were moved immediately. What were the values and beliefs held by some AFP officers behind this behaviour?
>
> • That women were seen as a safety risk to their partners in dangerous situations and therefore no good as police;
>
> • That because some magistrates won't convict members of the public for swearing at police in public, female police shouldn't complain about swearing and bad behaviour at the station but they should put up with it like all police put up with it on the street;
>
> • That during demonstrations, police women must be prepared to be manhandled by crowds and, therefore, at the station they should be able to "cop it sweet" if they are "man handled";
>
> • That sexual harassment doesn't happen here. "If only someone" the joke goes, "would sexually harass me!"
>
> • That you don't complain about a brother officer, no matter what happens;
>
> • That if you can't take the heat you should get out of the kitchen and, finally,
>
> • It's not safe to complain because you won't be taken seriously.

Commissioner Palmer made a strong commitment to implementing the reforms recommended by Niland.[53] These included enhanced training in equity and diversity principles; a program to reduce harassment including through better complaint resolution procedures; enlargement of flexible employment options; the adoption of targets such as women in 20% of management positions; and a plan to ensure policies were implemented across AFP regions.[54] Although, as noted, at the end of the 1990s the AFP numbers were not outstanding, they did show ongoing improvement.

Conclusion

The 1990s were marked by a shift away from police management discretion in matters of equity. New laws placed legal obligations on police that made their entrenched practices of discrimination and harassment technically illegal. But due to an appallingly weak enforcement apparatus, compliance with the new anti-discrimination and equal opportunity laws was inconsistent and still very much reliant on the discretion of police leaders. A minority were able to avoid their obligations in a crude manner; while others avoided, or failed to understand, the full implications of the spirit of the legislation. The stand out cases of successful resistance were Victoria and Western Australia, where numerous barriers to women remained, most notably military-style physical tests in recruitment and unmitigated discrimination and harassment on the job. By the end of the decade, a series of exposés and successful law suits forced the Victorian Police Commissioner to institute change. Change was about to come to Western Australia as well.

Chapter 5

A Brave New Century

The 1990s were marked by a strong divergence between police departments in the way in which senior managers, especially commissioners, responded to the new imperatives of equity legislation. At the very end of the 1990s this changed, and a clear convergent trend was confirmed. The principal cause of this change was the appointment of new commissioners who were willing to move with the times and apply key principles contained in equity legislation. By 2015, one hundred years after the appointment of the first policewomen, the formal barriers to women in policing had been largely dismantled, although evidence remained of a cultural lag in attitudes and some practices. A common system of non-discrimination in human resource management, with some moderate affirmative action measures, was apparent in every jurisdiction.

The effects of applying the new equity laws were most evident in recruitment. By the early-2000s, residual barriers against women (and some men) — such as military-style obstacle course tests in recruitment — had been moderated or eliminated. Where numbers were available, female applicants and female recruits averaged around one-third. By 2014, women also made up over one-quarter of sworn officers. They were concentrated in the lower ranks but there was a steady, if very slow, upwards movement. A number of women made it to the executive level of police departments. On a less positive note, it appeared that recruit numbers were stuck around a third, at best, with overall female numbers also likely to peak around a third or less by about 2020. There was also evidence of a retention issue, with women leaving policing before retirement at a higher rate than men. The reasons for this were unclear. Did women face more acute problems of work–life balance, or were women exercising their freedom and leaving policing for other opportunities?

The Underachievers

When Barry Matthews was appointed Police Commissioner in Western Australia in June 1999, he was quick to declare his commitment to improving the position of women and began working with the Office of Equal Employment Opportunity. Female recruit numbers and sworn officer numbers very slowly began to catch up with the other jurisdictions. In 2001, Matthews set up a Women's Advisory Network, reporting directly to him, and also engaged the University of Western Australia in a study on gender equity within the Force. The report was blunt in its main findings:[1]

> The reference Group has encountered, discussed, analysed and been shocked by the continuing level of unlawful practices that women in this service are subjected to in their daily working lives. The unlawful practices range from sexist comments through to threats of sexual assault. These practices begin at Recruitment School and continue through to senior levels. The perpetrators are known, are at all levels, and many have been promoted, and continue to be promoted.

The report's release in 2003 was described in detail as follows in an Australian Associated Press report:[2]

> Female officers in the West Australian Police Service were subjected to systemic discrimination and harassment at the hands of dinosaurs and bullies, a new report has found ...

> The report ... found that many policewomen were subject to daily 'hostility, discrimination, harassment and bullying'.

> "Both men and women interviewed for these projects have applied a variety of names to the males who engage in these behaviours, including dinosaurs, thugs and bullies," the report stated.

> UWA researcher Susan Harwood said the report also showed women were disproportionately under-represented in terms of promotion, and those who had risen through the ranks felt they were under greater scrutiny than their male colleagues.

> WA has Australia's lowest proportion of female police at 17.4%.

> Of those only four have been promoted to the rank of senior sergeant, and three to the rank of inspector ...

> Commissioner Barry Matthews said the report identified a poor police culture that was not supportive of women, showed unsworn women were not receiving enough training, and that female recruits were 'in some ways groomed for subservient roles in policing'.

> "I'm not pleased that that's confirmed what we've suspected but on the other hand I am pleased that we have had the courage to lift up the rock, find out

what the problem is, identify it and start doing something about it," Mr Matthews said.

He said in response to the findings of the report, former policewomen would be encouraged to return to the service, training opportunities for unsworn women would be improved and mentoring support for women would be extended.

A 'robust exit process' would also identify women on the verge of quitting the service and offer them greater support.

"We do want women to pay a greater role as leaders of the police, and our police service should as far as possible endeavour to reflect the diversity of our community," Mr Matthews said.

Despite these developments, Western Australia is notable for an ongoing struggle to meet reasonable expectations about women's representation in policing — despite overt political support. The following report from a Perth news outlet in 2013 epitomises this convergence of a common language around EEO, including police and politicians, with an acknowledgement of ongoing problems:[3]

New campaign to attract more female, multicultural police

ASHLEE MULLANY, PERTHNOW NOVEMBER 16, 2013 10:44AM

WA Police have launched a new advertising campaign to boost the number of female and multicultural recruits.

Premier Colin Barnett today launched the new TV, radio and print advertisements, which call for more women to 'step forward' into policing.

WA has one of the lowest rates of female police officers in the country — with about 1200 women in the ranks compared to about 4650 men.

It's hoped the $1 million advertising push will lift the rate from 21% to the national average of 25%.

Mr Barnett said the recruitment drive was part of an election commitment to deliver 550 new police officers over the next four years.

Police Inspector Kim Travers said the 'glass ceiling' in policing had been 'smashed'.

"We would encourage women in particular and people

from culturally diverse backgrounds to step forward," Insp Travers said.

"The glass ceiling as we have often heard has been absolutely smashed in WA Police. We have officers at the Assistant Commissioner level, at superintendent level, at inspector level making key decisions on your behalf.

"I've had an amazing career and I would encourage anyone who is thinking of representing their community to have the courage and conviction to stand up."

Mr Barnett said police were also committed to recruiting more Aboriginal officers.

"It is very important that WA Police reflects the community it serves," he said.

In Victoria, the law eventually caught up with Comrie and his cronies. The Narell McKenna case, and other exposés, provoked a group of women to form 'Operation Womenforce', which began a campaign 'to combat the perceived institutionalised harassment, neglect and negation of women police in Victoria'.[4] In 1999, Comrie was forced into a public mea culpa, admitting Victoria Police had not done enough to address discriminatory behaviour while launching an equity program to 'catch up with community standards'.[5] The new program was described as follows:[6]

> [T]he Equal Employment Opportunity Unit would be integrated within the Chief Commissioner's office, a new Managing Diversity and Respecting Individuality Policy would be established and a promotional campaign targeting women launched.
>
> More flexible arrangements for women with children will be introduced and a carer's room set up at the Victorian Police Centre so parents can care for children when other arrangements have fallen through.

Another newspaper report in December 1999 provided some detail on practical changes in Victoria:[7]

Police Policy Overhaul Lowers
The Barriers to Women Recruits

Women have faced many barriers in their attempts to join the police. Some of them have been literal.

Take the size of the fence in the recruits' agility course:

since it was lowered earlier this year to the average Victorian fence height, the female pass rate has jumped from less than half to 80% .

Then there's the dog squad, which has never had a female member. Ms Kathy Ettershank, the force's manager for equity and diversity, said that until recently it had been thought that women were not strong enough to carry a dog — something squad members are not required to do anyway.

They're just two examples, according to the Victoria Police, of how the organisation is overhauling its policies to ensure that women and members of minority groups — from gays and lesbians to Aborigines and Torres Strait Islanders — get a better go.

(Women) comprise only 14% of Victoria's police officers, the second lowest figure in the country. Even fewer rise to senior positions — just 1.5% of police inspectors are female ...

The chief commissioner, Mr Neil Comrie, insists that the force is committed to changing its ways.

Mr Comrie and the rest of the senior command have just finished a 10-week training course in which the speakers included policewomen telling horror stories of their experiences on their job.

They also heard the Attorney-General, Mr Rob Hulls, lecture them on the need to pay more than lip service to equal opportunity and diversity questions.

Some sessions may have caused personal discomfort to some of the command, Mr Comrie admitted this week, and it would take a while for the culture of such a large organisation to change. But he can already point to encouraging data.

The percentage of female recruits has jumped from around 20% last year to about 30% , partly based on the changes to the agility course (the length of time allowed to complete the course has also increased by half a minute).

The new blood means police expect their overall female numbers to rise to 16% next year — a small improvement, admits Ms Ettershank, but the start of something bigger. Then there are the less tangible cultural changes.

> The heads of the force's elite squads, from the special operations group to search and rescue, have been asked to identify any barriers or rules or, just as crucially, entrenched attitudes, which discourage women and members of minority groups from joining.
>
> The force's assistant director of human resources, Mr Gary Glover, emphasises that this does not mean weakening the squads' entrance standards. It's more about finding practices, such as the unnecessarily high wall in the pursuit course that are not relevant to practical police experience ...
>
> Mr Comrie said he had no illusions about the work to be done, but he warned recalcitrant police that there could be no turning back.
>
> 'I've seen no sign of any resistance — in fact, quite a deal of enthusiasm. To put it bluntly, though, if some of our members are either unable or unwilling to go with us, then we will be telling them: "There is no place for you at this organisation".'

There was a long way to go, even with a born again Chief Commissioner leading the charge. The replacement of Comrie with Christine Nixon in 2001 assured the securing of these initiatives. But there was still going to be a long uphill battle. In 2003, as one example, *The Sunday Age* revealed that the Victoria Police had spent over $1million of taxpayers' money over the previous three years settling bullying, harassment and discrimination claims from employees.[8] The newspaper referred to 'a continuing pattern of payouts following the landmark 1998 $125,000 Anti-Discrimination Tribunal payout to former Bairnsdale police officer Narell McKenna', and challenged police to reveal the details of the secret payouts. A Police Association spokesperson reportedly stated that five female police officers had been the recipients of confidential payments in the previous 18 months over discrimination and harassment claims. A lawyer was also cited:[9]

> [H]e had helped negotiate at least eight cases brought by gay and lesbian police between 2000 and 2002. All were settled through the force's internal Equity and Diversity Unit, with payouts ranging from $20,000 to $90,000. Just over half the cases involved lesbian complainants.

"They suffered from both misogyny and homophobia," Mr Trueman said. 'The police is a boys' club. We've had 25 years of equal opportunity at Victoria Police and we're still far from getting it right'.

In late-2014, Victorian Chief Commissioner of Police Ken Lay was obliged to establish an internal taskforce, and requested the assistance of the Victorian Equal Opportunity and Human Rights Commission, to investigate ongoing problems of sex sexual harassment. According to one media report:[10]

(The Commissioner) said the investigation was sparked by the 'reprehensible' behaviour of some members of the organisation.

The Chief Commissioner said there were currently a number of investigations underway into the 'shameless conduct by some of our people'.

"There are some men in this organisation whose behaviour towards women is reprehensible," he said.

"It is based on a sense of entitlement by some men, who think it's okay to sexually harass, intimidate, and degrade women.

"The behaviour is simply unacceptable and has no relationship to our sworn duty to uphold the right."

Since 2011, Victoria Police have received 20 allegations of sexual harassment.

Mr Lay said a number of investigations were underway into complaints, including of women being filmed in change rooms and simulated sexual acts performed at work.

Two Victoria Police employees have already been dismissed, two fined, one demoted and two have been suspended over incidents of sexual harassment, he said.

Onwards and Upwards: 2003/04 to 2007/08

The final national study, referred to in the previous chapter, covered the five years from 2003/04 to 2007/08.[11] The findings were again mixed but supported the picture of a general convergence in staffing profiles and equity practices. At the same time, the study highlighted the ongoing lack of consistent and comprehensive data, and the associated problems of highly inadequate transparency and accountability. Overall, the number of sworn female officers continued to trend upwards slowly, with an increase at the national level from 21.7% in 2003/04 to 24.3% in 2007/08. The rate of increase on average was 0.6% per annum. Behind these figures there was, again, considerable jurisdictional variation, as shown in table 5.1. New South Wales had the highest number of fully sworn officers on record, with 26.3%. Western Australia had the lowest percentage at 19.7%, but this was up from a very low based of 16.0%. The largest change was in Victoria, with an increase from 18.9% to 23.4%. There was a mysterious reduction of 2.3% in the Federal Police, down to 22.0%.

Table 5.1 Sworn Female Officers, Australia and New Zealand

Jurisdiction	2003/04 % Women Police	2007/08 % Women Police	% Change
Australian Federal Police	24.29	22.00	-2.29
New South Wales	24.52	26.38	+1.86
Northern Territory*	29.00	28.20	-0.80
Queensland	21.81	25.10	+3.29
South Australia	22.91	24.20	+1.29
Tasmania	22.81	26.04	+3.23
Victoria	18.94	23.48	+4.54
Western Australia	16.04	19.73	+3.69
Australia Total	21.78	24.30	+1.46

Note: 2007–2008: Total female N Australia = 13, 868, total female N New Zealand = 1, 449.
* Includes Aboriginal Community Police Officers (ACPOs) and auxiliary officers.

Recruit numbers were only available for four departments. In 2007/08, Tasmania had 42.0% female recruits, Victoria 40.0%, Queensland 33.6% and South Australia 27.9%. There were declines in three of the four departments, suggesting that female recruitment had peaked around a third nationally. Available numbers for rank are shown in tables 5.2 and 5.3. Table 5.2 has ranks collapsed into broad bands. The Australian Federal Police (AFP) ranks are reportedly separately because of their completely different system. Again, considerable variation is apparent with a general upward trend.

Table 5.4 combines data from 2003/04 to 2007/08, and shows total male and female applications for promotion, as well as promotion numbers, for three departments that supplied data. Significantly more females were successful in their applications in New South Wales (+4.67%) and Tasmania (+8.57%). Departments provided data on harassment and discrimination complaints in quite different forms. Available data indicated very small numbers of formal notifications or complaints, although the large majority were made by women — averaging between 5 and 15 per annum in the larger

Table 5.2 Rank, Four Australian Jurisdictions and New Zealand

Rank	2003/04 % Female	2007/08 % Female	% Change
Northern Territory			
Executive and Commissioned Officers	16.33%	21.43%	+5.10%
Non-Commissioned Officers	9.36%	22.86%	+13.50%
Constables and Recruits[a]	22.34%	21.24%	-1.10%
Victoria			
Executive Officers	9.09%	18.18%	+9.09%
Commissioned Officers	3.64%	5.19%	+1.55%
Non-Commissioned Officers	6.54%	8.80%	+2.27%
Constables	17.85%	27.67%	+9.83%
Queensland			
Executive Officers	6.67%	13.33%	+6.67%
Commissioned Officers	6.29%	5.65%	-0.64%
Non-Commissioned Officers	9.73%	13.77%	+4.04%
Constables	27.47%	30.99%	+3.52%
South Australia			
Executive Officers	16.67%	22.22%	+5.56%
Commissioned Officers	4.76%	9.63%	+4.87%
Non-Commissioned Officers	7.29%	11.27%	+3.99%
Constables	26.74%	29.55%	+2.80%

Note: [a] Disaggregated figures not available.

Table 5.3 Rank, Australian Federal Police

Rank	2003–2004 % Female	2007–2008 % Female	% Change
Senior Executive Service	14.81%	12.24%	-2.57%
Band 1	0.00%	0.00%	0.00%
Band 2	27.68%	22.03%	-5.65%
Band 3	30.04%	23.69%	-6.35%
Band 4	26.60%	24.49%	-2.11%
Band 5	30.17%	21.33%	-8.84%
Band 6	20.43%	24.32%	+3.89%
Band 7	20.40%	20.41%	+0.01%
Band 8	20.41%	15.69%	-4.72%
Band 9	14.79%	15.47%	+0.68%

Table 5.4 Applications and Promotions, 2003/04 to 2007/08

Jurisdiction	% F Applications	% M Applications	% F Promotions	% M Promotions	Per cent Change
New South Wales	11.70% (2548)	88.30% (19,221)	16.37% (520)	83.63% (2656)	+4.67%
Tasmania[a]	8.30% (63)	91.70% (696)	16.87% (14)	83.13% (69)	+8.57%
Western Australia	9.45% (444)	90.55% (4255)	11.05% (102)	88.95% (821)	+1.60%

Note: [a] Data for Tasmania cover 4.5 years from 1/01/2004; M = Male; F = Female.

departments. Where information was available on outcomes, it seemed the majority of cases ended with an apology, informally or with 'no action taken'.

Five departments provided data on separations covering five years. The average male/female separation rate of 77.0/22.9 approximated the average male/female proportion of sworn officers at 75.8/24.2. Again, however, male officers were most likely to retire — and also die or be dismissed. Female officers had a resignation rate slightly higher than the male resignation rate. New South Wales included 'Resignation — Family/Domestic' as a reason for separating. Over the period, women made up 17.8% of all officers who separated and males made up 82.1%. For 'Resignation — Family/ Domestic', women were 38.8% ($n = 7$) and males were 61.1% ($n = 11$).

Data on deployment indicated a fairly wide distribution of women across a range of duty types and specialisations, as exemplified in Table 5.5 for Western Australia There were only a few cases of high levels of female representation in traditional roles, such as 'domestic violence and victim support liaison officer' or low levels of female representation in other areas — such as in 'tactical operations', 'duty officer', 'corporate service', 'dog section' and 'counter terrorism and state protection.'

The Data Problem ... Still

The study summarised in the previous section, published in 2010 and covering the period 2003/04 to 2007/08, was the last national study on the record that attempted to cover all the key dimensions of gender

Table 5.5 Female Deployment, Western Australia, 2003/04 to 2007/08

Role	% F	% M
Total Sworn Officers	18.28	81.72
Administration	21.86	78.14
Corruption Prevention and Investigation	15.73	84.27
Counter Terrorism and State Protection	9.40	90.60
Metropolitan Support	19.03	80.97
North Metropolitan Region	19.06	80.94
Regional WA Region	16.80	83.20
South Metropolitan Region	20.70	79.30
Specialist Crime	12.52	87.48
State Intelligence	31.21	68.79
Traffic and Operations	15.83	84.17

Note: *Average total police over 5 years N = 5,235.*

equity in policing. This was an ad hoc study carried out by academics in a university. Today, there is still no source for vital statistics on gender equity in Australian policing, current and over time. This is a national disgrace and a clear failure of federal bodies charged with monitoring, coordinating and improving policing Australia-wide.

The last agency to provide a partial account of gender in policing was the Australian Institute of Criminology. The Institute provided regular reports on male and female numbers in policing by rank up to 2006 —Table 5.6 and Table 5.7. However, it abandoned the reports because of increasing differences in police systems. The AFP adopted its unique rank structure and New South Wales did away with the traditional Academy recruit system. Interested parties now have to trawl through eight police annual reports (not including the New South Wales Crime Commission or the Australian Crime Commission) to find some numbers on gender in policing. All the annual reports have large gaps. Bizarrely, the 'Premier State' does not even list numbers of sworn male and female officers.[17]

The most recent nationally consistent data are from the 2011 census, although they are not available by jurisdiction. Table 5.8 shows the results, including for the 2006 census as a point of comparison, as categorised by the Australian Bureau of Statistics. It would appear that women most likely reached the one quarter mark as a per-

Table 5.6: Australian Policing x Jurisdiction & Gender, 2006[18]

Jurisdiction	Male		Female		n
	n	%	%	%	
New South Wales	10,895	74	3,739	26	14,634
Victoria	8,854	79	2,321	21	11,175
Queensland	7,128	67	2,141	23	9,269
Western Australia	4,073	81	888	19	5,311
South Australia	3,192	77	976	23	4,168
Tasmania	937	75	309	25	1,246
Northern Territory	717	72	194	28	1,182
Australian Capital Territory	489	79	133	21	622
Australia	*36,285*	*77*	*10,701*	*23*	*46,986*

Table 5.7 Australian Police Services Combined x Rank and Gender, 2006[19]

	Male		Female		n
	n	%	%	%	
Sworn personnel					
Senior executive 1	78	90	9	10	87
Superintendent	380	92	32	8	412
Inspector	1,364	92	111	8	1,475
Senior sergeant	1,786	91	168	9	1,954
Sergeant 3	7,678	89	992	11	8,683
Senior constable	15,035	76	4,672	24	19,707
Constable 4	9,343	67	4,495	33	13,838
Probationary constable	616	73	222	27	838
External secondments	5	100	0	0	5
Total	*36,285*	*77*	*10,701*	*23*	*46,986*
Unsworn personnel					
Recruits	607	65	324	35	931
Cadets	51	61	32	39	83
Police aides 5	110	46	131	54	241
ACPO/Spec. constable 6	77	71	31	29	108
Other 7	140	84	26	16	166
Public service employee 8	4,169	33	8,323	67	12,492
Other personnel 9	448	49	463	51	911
Total	*41,886*	*68*	*20,031*	*32*	*61,917*

Table 5.8 Australia Census: Male and Female Police Officers, 2006 and 2011[20]

Category	2006				2011			
	Male	Female	Persons	Female %	Male	Female	Persons	Female %
139113 Commissioned Police Officer	759	65	824	7.87	715	75	790	9.49	+1.62
441311 Detective	1,942	426	2,368	17.98	2,119	630	2,749	22.91	+4.93
441312 Police Officer	31,627	10,074	41,701	24.15	34,709	11,998	46,707	25.68	+1.53
441300 Police nfd*	37	24	61	39.34	65	23	88	16.12	+1.73
Total	34,365	10,589	44,954	23.55	37,608	12,726	50,334	25.28	

Note: * Not further defined

centage of all officers in 2010. The final column on the right shows the percentage increases over time, indicating very small upward growth overall and at the commissioned officer level, but with a larger increase of almost 5% in the detective category to 22.9% — not far below the overall per cent.

Christine Nixon

This census data showed approximately 9.5% of women in policing at the level of Inspector or above in 2011. The 1990s and 2000s were critical for the entry of women into senior management positions. In the 21st century, more women appeared in commissioner and deputy commissioner positions. Christine Nixon is, of course, the stand out woman in modern Australian policing. Her appointment as Chief Commissioner in Victoria in 2001 was the crowning glory of an impressive career.[21] In Victoria, she was in charge of a force with over 12,000 personnel. She had already achieved a great deal in New South Wales, rising to the rank of Assistant Commissioner in charge of Human Resources in 1994, after joining in 1972. Her time as Assistant Commissioner included the turmoil of Wood Royal Commission into police corruption (1994–97). As an outsider to Victoria Police, and a woman, she faced the prospect of opposition and resistance at every turn. Her efforts at creating a more consultative and supportive organisational culture were welcomed by many and she quickly achieved a very high level of popularity and support across Victorian society and within the Victoria Police.[22] Nixon adopted a problem-solving philosophy of policing, and claimed a wide range of achievements in crime reduction and improved police–community relations. She admittedly struggled to get on top of the perennial problems of corruption, violence and sexism in the Force. One muckraking journalist accused her of having 'feminised' the Victorian Police Force,[23] apparently blindly ignorant to the fact that this was exactly what the Force needed.

Very sadly, Christine Nixon's latter years in Victoria were marred by some highly personalised conflicts. The police union leadership and rivals in senior management were always on the lookout for opportunities to attack. She was roundly condemned for an ill-advised all expenses paid trip to Los Angeles on an inaugural Qantas Airbus flight in 2008. And she was brutally attacked over the maintenance of her policy of delegation during the 2009 Black Saturday bushfires.[24] She had already planned to leave the police before the fires, and she subsequently took on the job of chair of the Victorian Bushfire Reconstruction and Recovery Authority.

Australasian Council for Women and Policing

A major step forward in the professional development of women police in Australia occurred with the establishment of the Australasian Council for Women and Policing (ACWAP) in 1997. The council was formed following the inaugural Women and Policing Conference held in Sydney in 1996. The conference was an initiative of Melinda Tynan, a New South Wales police officer, and Helen McDermott, a public servant in the AFP. The inaugural ACWAP Committee comprised:[25]

- President: Christine Nixon, NSW Police Service
- Vice President: Melinda Tynan, NSW Police Service
- Secretary: Helen McDermott, Australian Federal Police
- Treasurer: Pam Robson, Queensland Police Service
- Ordinary committee members: Denise Burke and Jacki Drew, Queensland Police Service; Linda Waugh, Criminal Justice Commission, Queensland.

The council operates largely as a support group for women police. The premier event is the conference, which includes delegates from around the world, including subsidised delegates from police forces in developing nations in the Asia–Pacific region. A commendable aspect of the ACWAP, and the conferences, captured in the name, is the wider focus on the prevention of crimes against women and improved policing services for women.

In 1998, ACWAP published the first issue of its magazine *The Journal for Women and Policing*, which promotes women's career development and strategies to reduce the criminal victimisation of women. The inaugural editorial committee members were Denise Burke, Helen McDermott, Pam Robson and Melinda Tynan.[26] Another valuable innovation was the annual awards, which recognise outstanding service in areas related to women and policing. The bravery awards are an emotional highlight of the conference. The ACWAP also conducts development seminars, provides scholarships for career development purposes, and has input into various policy reviews in different jurisdictions.

The council's current vision is expressed as follows, to:[27]

- improve the policing services provided to women
- improve the opportunities and outcomes for women within policing
- participate in the global network of women in policing.

Apart from the conference, journal and awards, its activities include 'Keeping members informed through an email discussion list, and providing advice and data to a range of stakeholders, researchers and students'. In February 2015 the Executive and Management Team comprised:[28]

- President: Carlene York (NSW)
- Vice President: Katarina Carroll (QLD)
- Secretary: Deb Platz (QLD)
- Assistant Secretary: Annie McDonald (QLD)
- Treasurer: Ingrid Kuster (ACT)
- Assistant Treasurer: Julie Crabbe (QLD)
- Public Officer: Kylie Flower (AFP)
- Journal Editor: Phil Green (VIC)
- Committee Members: Melissa Hawkins (NSW) Social Media and Communication, Joanne Howard (SA), Denby Eardly (NSW), Susan Harwood (WA), Lyn Kaesler (NSW), Dorothy McPhail (NZ), Kim Eaton (QLD), Betty Green (NSW), Leanne Lomas (AFP), Lisa McMeeken

(VIC), Michelle Plumpton (TAS), Andrew Loader (VIC), Andrea Quinn (AFP), David Eardley (NSW).

Conclusion

The late-1990s and 2000s saw the consolidation of equity policies and practices in policing in response to new legislation. There were still considerable jurisdictional differences and fluctuations in the extent to which prohibitions on discrimination and harassment were enforced, and the extent to which the affirmative action spirit of the new laws was operationalised. It some cases, the adoption of equity measures required the passing of dinosaur commissioners who had retained considerable discretion in the face of weak government enforcement of the law. But by the 2010s, a clear convergence had emerged, with all the more overt discriminatory barriers removed and a variety of supportive policies in place for women, including flexible employment options. On the whole, it appeared that women were recruited and promoted close to the rates at which they applied. Police managers spoke a common language that was gender inclusive. Women officers passed the one-quarter mark and, as far as could be ascertained, recruit numbers settled around one-third. A brave new world of gender equality in policing had arrived! At the same time, the extent to which equity was fully optimal remained very much open to debate. And the debate was plagued by a lack of comprehensive data — suggesting on-going tokenism and managerial disinterest in the fundamentals of gender equity.

Postscript

Understanding and Preventing Sex Discrimination in Policing

The history of women in Australian policing began with a protracted ideological struggle between women's welfare groups and chauvinist male political and police leaders. The initial success of the women police movement in opening policing to women quickly proved to be a hollow victory. The battle was won but the war was lost — for many decades to come. Women were allowed into policing in most states to support the Australian effort in the First World War, a war fought primarily on the other side of the planet in the interests of imperial elites whose insatiable colonial ambitions had brought them to blows in a new form of industrialised killing. As the flower of Australian youth was massacred in foreign fields, police forces on the home front faced acute labour shortages and a variety of intensified social problems on the streets of the capital cities. In this hot house environment, women and girls needed to be protected from the predations of men, including the troops, but the fighting ability of the troops also needed to be protected from women who might be carrying diseases.[1]

Policing was just one more front in the battle between the sexes in which patriarchy dominated. Men won the battle for job security, power and occupational privileges within policing by using law to exclude or circumscribe women. This was part of a wider process which confined women to low paid service occupations or to unpaid home duties in the nuclear family supporting a dominant male. The closure of opportunities by law and regulations was buttressed by ideological opposition which located women's natural role in the home. Where a space was grudgingly made for female police, initially it was made only for spinsters and widows, and was merely as an extension of the conventional roles of nurturer and assistant. The women police movement itself was ambivalent about the extent to which women should perform the full range of police duties.[2]

Women police were also part of a battle over how policing was done. Janis Appier saw in the women police movement of the first half of the twentieth century a 'preventive-protective' model of policing fundamentally at odds with a 'punitive' or 'crime control' model.[3] The marginalisation of policewomen in small units also represented a minor concession and a major victory of the male dominated control model over the preventive model advocated by the women police movement. The war analogy allowed men to justify an exclusive domain for themselves based on arguments about physical ability in the war against crime.

The new women police were appointed in tiny numbers — two here, three there — until another global conflict created opportunities for very limited expansion. But even after World War Two, policewomen's duties largely remained those of social workers on the beat, serving also as assistants to detectives when female decoys, undercover operatives or typists were needed. There are two views about the larger effect of this work. The pessimistic 'social control' view was summed up in Leonie Stella's account of the early years of women police in Western Australia:[4]

> This 'welfare' work was in practice surveillance of women, particularly young women suspected of being 'immoral' and likely to spread venereal disease. Although the women police did carry out welfare duties which protected and assisted some women and children, particularly neglected children, the restriction on their duties together with the fact that they were primarily appointed as 'morals police' resulted in them interfering in the lives of working class women rather than assisting those who were victims of sexual crimes committed by me.

The evidence reviewed for this book suggests that something larger and more positive occurred through the employment of women police in Australia, mainly in the assistance and protection female officers provided to women and girls in trouble and danger. Much of this work has been subsumed by modern welfare agencies, but even today police provide the most visible frontline government service with a 24-hour seven-day-a-week patrol and rapid response capability with a mixed law enforcement/welfare orientation. One of Queensland's first female officers, Zara Dare, left behind a brief description of her work, emphasising its welfare role:

> I have been trying to teach the things I taught in China to the women and children who come in off the streets to the police courts. Every year policewomen in this city are responsible for bringing in hundreds of children from the streets who have been sent out to 'lift' goods from the chain stores. We bring them into the station, talk to them and take them home. We patrol the gardens and parks, the department stores and places of amusement. We try to be kind as well as just. Sometimes kindness is mistaken for weakness. I have taken many a 'hiding' in my time, but if I

have helped to lift a few people to their feet, given them any sort of incentive to run straight, it has all been in a very good cause.

Victim support and recognising offender victimisation were always central tenets of the policewomen philosophy, summed up in part in the term 'preventive justice'.[5] This approach is also illustrated in the following extract from an interview with two former Queensland policewomen from the 1940s and 1950s.

> *The missing girls, when you found them, would they usually go quietly?*
> Yes, because we always sided with them.
> *They wouldn't run?*
> No, they were glad to be brought to heel I suppose and then if they wanted to go home they usually could. If their parents couldn't control them, they were charged as uncontrollable before the children's court.
> We had to get off the streets quietly and everyone avoided confrontation.
> *You never felt you were forcing the girls into something worse?*
> No.
> No.
> We always took them back to the office and encouraged them. They used to come back with their babies when they got married and saw us as friends.
> *So a lot of them would come back?*
> Yes, not to the men so much.
> *So they felt you had rescued them?*
> Yes. It was the human touch.
> They treated us as their friends.[6]

A number of factors led to the gradual emergence of women police from their very confined world. The pioneer women benefitted from a chivalry factor. In the main, their competence and conservatism endeared them to their male colleagues. In fact, many female police ended up marrying their colleagues — and subsequently had to resign. Police rank-and-file acceptance of female officers produced a positive response to their requests to join the powerful police unions. Union membership led to a snowball process of industrial support for equal pay, equal powers and other rights. At the same time, the quirky agendas of police commissioners, in areas such as the deployment of women on road safety duties, added to the case for equal powers, uniforms and assignment to general duties.

Overarching all this from the 1960s was the tidal wave effect of the second wave of feminism, which created an environment in which it was felt that women could do anything and women were encouraged into every field of human endeavour. As women police proved they could work as detectives, manage police stations and take on the rigours of frontline police work — even die in the service of the community — individuals broke through barriers and paved the way for more and more conquests of privileged male spaces in policing. Women police benefitted from the introduction of superannuation and maternity leave in public sector employment — driven by the feminist movement. Despite these achievements, numerous barriers remained: quotas, marriage bars, an ideology of full-time careerism, discretionary decision making exercised against women in assignment and promotion, inappropriate physical tests, and unchecked harassment and ostracism on the job. (Many male officers and aspiring police also suffered from many of these impediments.)

In the end, police were forced to play fair by the wave of anti-discrimination and public sector equity legislation phased in from the 1970s to the 1990s. Even then, many resisted — avoiding compliance, doing as little as possible or creating bogus physical tests to exclude women from their special domain. Eventually the law triumphed, at least in the letter of the law if not the spirit. As the 21st century progressed, policing in Australia was finally free of formal institutionalised biases. The wash up in 2015 was a female complement around one quarter, women in all areas of policing, women moving up the ranks (making up 10% of commissioned officers); and recruit intakes around one third.

It had taken a century, and there had been hundreds of thousands of victims of police chauvinism: all the women turned away from a career in policing; all the women who got in but were treated like second class citizens or worse in many cases; all the men, women and children caught up in the criminal justice system, as victims or offenders, who needed a more compassionate and reasonable response from police.

The turn of the century signalled a whole new world of opportunity for women in police work. However, the exact direction of that future remains uncertain. Too many women were leaving well before retirement. Was this a good thing — exercising their freedom, seeking new experiences; or a bad thing — suffering burnout, leaving an inflexible organisation? Would parity or better ever be reached?

The roots of all the prejudice documented in this book are not hard to understand. Pioneering researchers, like Jennifer Hunt, who engaged in participant observation data collection, showed that women police not only threatened the lucrative employment domain monopolised by men but challenged the mythology of policing that gives it its special status: that policing requires tough masculine qualities.[7] It was a job for male heroes that only hard men could do. But there was also another, much more sinister side, to male fanaticism about keeping out women. For whatever reason — nature or nurture — female police had more integrity than most male police. The presence of women police challenged networks of corruption that flourished in the traditional culture of closed policing organisations, exempted from political scrutiny and accountability.[8] As the new female officers at Darlinghurst police station discovered in the 1970s, male officers on the take, who exercised a free hand in bashing suspects or sexually exploiting women, felt uncomfortable when female officers were around. Women were a disruptive force, a force for a more moral policing.

There is one more reason that should be mentioned when it comes to (briefly) explaining sex discrimination in policing. For much of its history, Australian policing, as in many other locations, was characterised by ignorance and habit over science. There were many casualties of a reactionary approach to the task and the promotion to senior management of some of the most ignorant and uneducated public servants in the country. There was a massive failure to protect victims of crime. There was a tragic failure to protect police officers from the physical, psychological and moral hazards of the job. And there was a sustained, intergenerational, prejudice about women which was completely at odds with the evidence. The 1970s saw a series of highly innovative performance studies in the United States comparing male and female police.[9] Some of these studies found their way into policing in Australia but with no replication. The overseas studies indicated that women were not only as good at policing as men, but on a number of key indicators they were better — including in defusing conflict, resolving issues without resort to force, and assisting victims of crime. Recent research has only confirmed this picture, including academic Australian research.[10] The obvious conclusion from the science of gender and police performance is that more women — carefully selected, trained and supported — equals better policing.

How can sex discrimination in policing be eliminated and a better environment for women created in order to optimise women's careers and contributions to police work? It's easy. The research is very clear on this,[11] and a number of organisations have published very useful guides, including the Geneva Center for the Democratic Control of Armed Forces.[12] The first step involves eliminating all non bona fide employment criteria: quotas; height limits; arbitrary age limits; silly military-style obstacle course tests, ridiculous spatial reasoning tests, full-time employment requirements, obsessions with physical ability in training. These need to be replaced by scientifically grounded selection criteria in areas such as education, trainability, long-term health prospects, communication and problem solving skills, and mental health. The second step involves encouraging women to participate at all levels of policing: through recruitment campaigns aimed at women that include factual information about policing (e.g., it's much less dangerous than many occupations), mentoring programs, equity support officers, flexible employment options (which benefit men as well), inclusive selection panels, training in equity principles and evidence about gender and policing, and carrying out research designed to identify and counter barriers to women's full participation. The third step involves some good old law enforcement: prosecute sex pests and bigots in policing, make them unwelcome and drive them out.

Endnotes

Queensland policewoman Jocelyn Hartigan 1992.

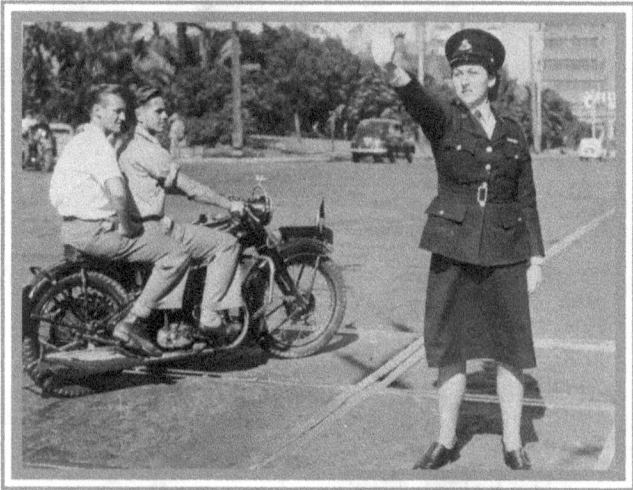

Amy Millgate directs traffic at the corner of Park and College streets, Sydney, 1948.

Chapter 1

1 C. Owings, 1969, *Women Police: A Study of the Development and Status of the Women Police Movement*, Patterson Smith, Montclair NJ.

2 Ibid.

3 Saturday, 14 June, p. 40.

4 Monday, 30 June 1913, p. 14.

5 Owings, op. cit.; P. Higgs and C. Bettess, 1987, *To Walk a Fair Beat: A History of the South Australian Women Police*, Past & Present Policewomen's Association, Adelaide, ch. 1; J. Appier, 1992, *Preventive Justice: The Campaign for Women Police, 1910–1940*, Women and Criminal Justice, 4(1), pp. 3–36.

6 Owings, op. cit., pp. 101ff, ch. 1.

7 The Centre for Policing Research, 1998, *Into the Blue: A Celebration of 80 Years for Women in Policing in Western Australia*, Edith Cowan University, Perth, p. 2.

8 Owings, op. cit.; L.A. Jackson, 2104, *The First World War and the First Female Police Officer*. Retrieved from https://history. blog.gov.uk/2014/06/17/the-first-world-war-and-the-first-female-police-officer/.

9 D. Potter, n.d., *The First Fifty Years in the History of the National Council of Women of Queensland*, Brisbane, p. 19.

10 C. Woolley, 1997, *Arresting Women: A History of Women in the Victoria Police*, Victoria Press, 1997, p. 1.

11 Ibid.

12 Ibid.

13 V. Kelly, 1961, *Rugged Angel: Australia's First Policewoman*, Angus & Robertson, Sydney, p. 6.

14 Ibid.

15 B. Swanton, 1983, Women Police in NSW — The Formative Years, *Australian Police Journal*, Oct–Dec; 141–142, 162, 165, 167; p. 144.

16 Ibid, p. 141.

17 Ibid, p. 7.

18 Ibid, p. 142.

19 Kelly, op. cit., p. 7.

20 Swanton, op. cit., p. 142; based on personal communication with ex DI June Kelly.

21 Saturday 21 March 1914, p. 7.

22 Sunday 12 April 1914, p. 28.

23 E.g., *Northern Star*, Thursday 23 July 1914, p. 4; Mudgee *Guardian*, Thursday, 23 July 1914, p. 15.

24 Tuesday, 4 August 1914, p. 4.

25 http://www.parliament.nsw.gov.au/prod/parlment/members.nsf.

26 Friday, 7 May 1915, p. 33.

27 The Tamworth Daily Observer, Saturday 15 May 1915, p. 2; The Sydney Stock and Station Journal, 21 May 1915, p. 6.

28 Wednesday 2 June 1915, p. 3.

29 Saturday June 4 1915, p. 9.

30 Swanton, p. 142; *The Tamworth Daily Observer* (NSW), Monday, 14 June 1915, p 1.

21 Kelly, op. cit., pp. 7-8.

32 Swanton, op. cit., p. 142; based on personal communication with ex DI June Kelly.

33 Kelly, op. cit., pp. 9-10.

34 Wednesday, 15 October 1913, p. 13.

35 Saturday, 22 November 1913, p. 5S.

36 Higgs and Bettess, op. cit., p. 11.

37 Ibid.

38 Ibid.

39 Ibid.

40 Ibid, p. 12.

31 Ibid.

42 Wednesday 11 March 1914, p 15.

43 18 February, p. 7.

44 In The Register, 16 April 1915, p. 5.

45 Monday 5 January 1914, p. 17.

46 Saturday 28 February 1914, p. 8.

47 In *The Register*, Wednesday 28 April 1915, p. 6.

48 *The Maitland Mercury*, 29 April 1915, p. 4.

49 Higgs and Bettess, op. cit., p. 13.

50 In ibid.

51 Ibid.

52 In ibid.

53 Ibid, p. 14.

54 Ibid.

55 Ibid.

56 Ibid, p. 17.

57 Ibid, p. 19.

58 Woolley, op. cit., p. 2.

59 Monday, 3 August 1914, p. 17.

60 In Woolley, op. cit., p. 2.

61 Ibid.

62 Ibid, p. 3.

63 In ibid.

64 In ibid.

65 In ibid.

66 In ibid, pp. 3-4.

67 Ibid, p. 4.

68 In ibid.

69 In ibid.

70 In ibid.

71 In ibid.

72 In ibid.

73 In ibid.

74 In ibid, p. 7.

75 Woolley, op. cit.; *Parliamentary Debates (Legislative Assembly)*, Vol. 143, 17 August 1916, p. 869.

76 In Woolley, op. cit., p. 7.

77 Ibid, p. 8.

78 Ibid.

79 *The Mercury*, 22 March 1917, p. 8.

80 E.g., *Police Annual Report*, 1917; Women Police, *Daily Post*, 31 July 1917, p. 4.

81 30 October 1917, p 4.

82 30 October 1917, p 4.

83 18 January 1918, No. 3052, p 1.

84 *Police Gazette*, Tasmania, December 6, 1918, No. 3098, p 1; Tasmania Police Force, 1974, *Brief History, 1804–1974*. Hobart, p 8.

85 N. Pink, 1979, 'Women's climb to the top of the police force', *The Mercury*, 18 January, p 13.

86 Ibid.

87 Centre for Policing Research Woolley, op. cit., p. 2.

88 8 November, p. 8.

89 7 February 1916, p. 4.

90 *The Daily News*, 7 February 1916, p. 4.

91 *The Police Review* (Western Australia), Vol. II, No. 15, 1917, p. 1.

92 Ibid.

93 Ibid.

94 Ibid, p. 2.

95 *The Police Review* (Western Australia), December 1917 (Vol. II, No. 20), p. 1.

96 L. Stella, 1990, *Policing Women: Women's Police in Western Australia 1917–1943*, Honours thesis, Murdoch University, Perth, p. 72.

97 p. 16.

98 *The Police Review* (Western Australia), November 1917, p. 11.

99 Ibid.

100 *The Police Review*, December 1917, vol. II, no. 20, pp. 1-2.

101 Potter, op. cit., p. 19.

102 Letter to John Huxham, 14 September 1915; State Archives.

103 *Queensland Parliamentary Debates,* 28 September 1915, pp. 950–951.

104 *Telegraph,* 14 September 1915.

105 *Daily Mail,* 19 March 1927; Letter, AFWV to Premier McCormack, 27 September 1927, State Archives.

106 *Telegraph,* 8 April 1929; Higgs & Bettess, op. cit.

107 Brisbane *Daily Mail,* 24 June 1915.

108 *Brisbane Courier,* 21 November 1928.

109 T*elegraph,* 8 April 1929.

110 9 April 1929.

111 Letter, 24 July 1929; State Archives.

112 R. Fitzgerald (1984) From 1915 to the Early 1980s: A History of Queensland, University of Queensland Press, Brisbane, p. 47, n 91.

113 *Brisbane Courier,* 19 November 1930.

114 *Queensland Police Union Journal,* 29 October 1930, pp. 22-23; *Brisbane Courier,* 3 November 1930.

115 W.R. Johnston, 1992, *The Long Blue Line: A History of Queensland to the Present Day,* Boolarong Press, Brisbane, p. 215.

116 Queensland *Police Union Journal,* 29 October 1930, p. 23.

117 Ibid., p. 18.

118 *The Courier-Mail,* 2 March 1940.

119 B.A. Osborn, 1997, *'I'm not Mad — I'm a Policewoman!': Historical Notes and Anecdotes of Women in Federal Policing,* Australian Federal Police Museum, Canberra, Foreword.

120 Ibid, p. 1.

121 Ibid.

122 Ibid, p. 2.

123 Ibid.

124 Ibid.

125 In ibid, p. 3.

126 Ibid, p. 5.

127 Letter, A/Superintendent of Police J.W. Stokes to Police Commissioner, New South Wales, December 30, 1957, JWS/JT; Territory Archives.

128 E.g., Memo, Director of Welfare H.C. Greiss to the Administrator, March 11, 1959, HCG.AF; Territory Archives.

129 Memo, January 28, 1958, JWS/JT; Territory Archives.

130 Northern Territory Police, Annual Report 1960/61, p. 7.

131 W.J. McLaren (n.d.). *The Northern Territory and its Police Forces, 1869–1978*, pp. 1379–1381.

132 Citation (*NT Police Journal*), December 1964, p. 26.

133 McLaren, op. cit., p. 1381.

Chapter 2

1 Higgs & Bettess, op. cit., p. 19.

2 Ibid, p. 13.

3 Ibid, p. 21.

4 Ibid, p. 23.

5 Woolley, op. cit., p. 9.

6 Ibid.

7 Ibid, p. 21

8 Stella, op. cit., p. 83.

9 In ibid, p. 92.

10 Ibid, p. 85.

11 *Police Gazette*, Tasmania, October 26, 1917, No. 3040, p 1.

12 January 18, 1918, No. 3052, p 1.

13 The Mercury, October 29, 1917, p 4; The Examiner, October 30, 1917, p 4.

14 9 February 1918, p. 6.

15 Letter from Commissioner to New Zealand Police Commissioner, 19 August 1933; State Archives.

16 Johnston, op. cit., p. 216.

17 Osborn, op. cit., p. 3.

18 Ibid, p. 7.

19 Kelly, op. cit., p. 10.

20 Ibid, p. 10.

21 In ibid, p. 11.

22 In ibid, pp. 11–12.

23 Ibid, p. 12.

24 Op. cit., pp. 29–30.

25 Ibid, p 31.

26 Ibid, p. 31.

27 In ibid, pp. 37–38.

28 *Women Police Journal*, Mt Gambier Police, Feb. 1926 – Mar. 1928, Vol. 3; GRG 5/151/21; State Records.

29 Women Police Journal, Mt Gambier Police, Mar. 1939 - Jan. 1941, Vol. 7; GRG 5/151/21; State Records.

30 Ibid.

31 Ibid.

32 Police Department: Report for 1918-19, Parliament of Tasmania, 1919, p. 7.

33 The Mercury, 1 May 1918, p. 3.

34 Stella, op. cit., p. vi.

35 Ibid, pp. 83–85.

36 Ibid, op. cit., pp. 86–87.

37 S. Sinclair,1964, *The Women Police: 1939–1961*, Thesis, Graylands Teachers' College, p. 6.

38 Letter from Commissioner to New Zealand Police Commissioner, 19 August 1933; State Archives.

39 Ibid.

40 9 March 1963.

41 Commissioner of Police: Report for Years 1933–34 to 1938–39, p. 3.

42 Kelly, op. cit., p. 13.

43 In ibid, p. 14.

44 In ibid, p. 18.

45 Ibid, chapter 4.

46 In ibid, p. 26.

47 Higgs and Bettess, op. cit., p. 27.

48 Ibid, p. 27.

49 Ibid, p. 28.

50 For Western Australia, see Stella, op. cit., chapter 3.

51 In Woolley, op. cit., p. 21.

52 In Woolley, op. cit., p. 23.

53 Letter from Commissioner to New Zealand Commissioner, 19 August 1933; State Archives.

54 Letters, 21 February and 7 April, State Archives (Commissioners' Correspondence).

55 18 April 1933.

56 Potter, op. cit., p. 19; *The Courier-Mail*, 16 September 1937; Carroll, Letter to Under Secretary, 5 October 1937, State Archives.

57 *The Telegraph*, 19 October 1937.

58 E.g., Stella, op. cit., chapter 3.

59 Informants 13–19.

60 K. Saunders and H. Taylor, 1987, The Impact of Total War Upon Policing: The Queensland Experience, in M. Finnane (Ed.), *Policing in Australia: Historical Perspectives*, New South Wales University Press, Kensington, p. 159.

61 30 June 1942.

62 Letter to Commissioner, 18 November 1942.

63 Informant 13.

64 Johnston, op. cit., p. 212.

65 Saunders and Taylor, op. cit., pp. 158–159.

66 Informants 13 and 14.

67 Letter to Commissioner New Zealand Police, 19 August 1933, State Archives.

68 *The Courier-Mail*, circa 4 March 1941.

69 Women Police, Qld Police Union submission to Qld Industrial Court, 1955, p. 17; State Archives.

70 Informants 13 and 14.

71 Informants 8–15.

72 Johnston, op. cit., p. 217.

73 'Police Award - State, Judgement', JP O'Malley, 5 October 1956, p. 2.

74 Informant 13.

75 Memo, sub-inspector to inspector CIB, 13 January 1955.

76 Telegram from Carroll to inquiry from New Zealand, 17 August 1943.

77 Informants 13 and 14.

78 *Centenary History*, 1963, QPF, Brisbane, pp. 61.

79 Comments by Risch on memo, Boyle to Risch, 26 September 1950.

80 *Sunday Mail*, 15 March 1953.

81 Informant 14.

82 Informants 2, 13, 14, 15; Qld Police Union submission to Qld Industrial Court in response to commissioner's objection, circa 14 December 1956, p. 13.

83 'Women Police', Qld Police Union submission to Qld Industrial Court, 1955, pp. 4–5.

84 Informant 13.

85 Ibid.

86 Letter, Minister for Police to the Secretary of the Labour Women's Central Executive, July 9, 1942; Western Australia Archive.

87 Op cit., p. 24.

88 Woolley, op. cit., p. 84.

89 Ibid, p. 85.

90 Ibid, p. 85.

91 Woolley, op. cit., p. 81.

92 Informant 37.

93 Interview with Tim Prenzler, 17 August 2010, Brisbane.

94 Minutes, Queensland Police Union Conference, 7–10 March, 1955, p. 30.

95 Informants 13 and 14.

96 'Police Award – State, Judgement', JP O'Malley, 5 October 1956, pp. 1–2, 4.

97 Letter, Commissioner Smith to Minister, 2 May 1950.

98 *Police Journal*, 30 September 1955, p. 9.

99 'Women Police', Qld Police Union submission to Qld Industrial Court, 1955.

100 Letter, solicitor-general, 24 September 1956; Tait, response to Application by the Queensland Police Union of Employees for Variation of the Police Award — State, 1956, pp. 5–13; 'Police Award — State, Judgement', JP O'Malley, 5 October 1956, p. 5.

101 'Police Award — State, Judgement', JP O'Malley, 5 October 1956, p. 5.

102 'Objection to Jurisdiction', Commissioner of Police, 27 September 1956.

103 'Police Award — State Judgement', JP O'Malley, 5 October 1956; Qld Police Union submission to Qld Industrial Court in response to commissioner's objection, circa 14 December 1956, p. 15.

104 'Police Award — State, Provision for Policewomen Judgement', L. Brown, 22 March 1957, pp. 1-5.

105 *Queensland Government Gazette*, 14, 13 May (1957), p. 240.

106 *Telegraph*, 21 March 1957.

107 Ibid, 28 March 1957.

108 *Truth*, 31 March 1957.

109 Informant 37.

110 27 March 1957.

Chapter 3

1 Tynan, 1948, p. 23; Why women traffic police were employed, *New South Wales Police News*, March, p. 32.

2 Tynan, op. cit., p. 23.

3 *Truth*, 11 August 1957.

4 M. Tynan, 1995, *80 Years of Women in Policing New South Wales 1915 to 1995*, New South Wales Police Service, Sydney, p. 6.

5 Ibid, p. 28.

6 Ibid, p. 28.

7 Ibid.

8 *New South Wales Police News*, April 1947, p. 8; May, p. 33.

9 Tynan, op. cit., p. 24

10 Ibid, p. 29.

11 Ibid, p. 21.

12 Ibid, p. 37.

13 C. Nixon and J. Chandler, 2012, *Fair Cop*, Victory Books, Melbourne.

14 Tynan, op. cit., p. 37.

15 Ibid, pp. 38–39.

16 'History of New South Wales Women in Policing', 2013, *The Journal for Women and Policing*, No. 11, p. 42.

17 'Chronicle of women police in SAPOL', 2013, *The Journal for Women and Policing*, No. 11, p. 37.

18 Ibid.

19 D. Purschee, 1984, 'The Police Partners Association', *Police Journal, SA*, 65(11), p. 33.

20 In *Police Journal, SA*, 1985, 66/11, p 18.

21 Woolley, op. cit.; E. St Johnston, 1971, *A Report on the Victoria Police Force*, Government Printer, Melbourne.

22 Woolley, op. cit., p. 153.

23 'History of AFP Women', 2013, *The Journal for Women and Policing*, No. 11, p. 38

24 *Women in Peacekeeping*, Third Australasian Women and Policing Conference: Women and Policing Globally, Canberra, 23 October 2002, p. 2.

25 'History of Women in the Western Australia Police Service', 2013, *The Journal for Women and Policing*, No. 11, pp. 43–44.

26 P. 7.

27 Report, Police Headquarters, Darwin, to Commissioner of Police, 11 November 1969. Territory Archives.

28 Nixon and Chandler, op. cit.

29 In Pink, op. cit., p 13.

30 C. Lidgard, 1988, *Women Policing in Australia.* Paper presented to the Annual Conference of the Sociological Association of Australia and New Zealand, Canberra, 29 November – 2 December, p. 2; T. Prenzler, 1994, *Women in the Queensland Police, 1931–1994,* Master of Arts thesis, University of Queensland, Brisbane, p. 20.

31 *The Mercury,* 8 June 1977.

32 *The Examiner,* 1 May 1976.

33 G. Ellsmore, Police cadet jobs — but not for girls, 16 November 1976, *The Mercury.*

34 *Women in the Police Force,* AA55/5, Archives Office of Tasmania.

35 Ibid.

36 Ibid.

37 P. Bloch, D. Anderson, and P. Gervais, 1973, *Policewomen on Patrol: Major Findings,* Police Foundation, Washington DC.

38 Letter, 29th June 1976; *Women in the Police Force,* AA55/5, Archives Office of Tasmania.

39 In Ellsmore, op cit.

40 13 February, In *Women in the Police Force,* AA55/5, Archives Office of Tasmania.

41 6 April, p 7.

42 E. Whinnett, 19, October 1996, The Thin Blue Line, *The Saturday Mercury,* p 36.

43 Ibid.

44 *Tasmania Police Journal,* 1970, June, p 6.

45 In *Tasmania Police Journal,* 1970, July, p 13.

46 Memo, Deputy Commissioner to Superintendent of Police, New Norfolk, 25 May 1971; see P1.13.77 Policewomen Visits to the West Coast 1967–1972, Archives Office of Tasmania.

47 Letter, Deputy Commissioner to Commissioner, 21 August 1957, Queensland State Archives.

48 Letter, Commissioner to Minister, 10 October 1957, State Archives.

49 *The Courier-Mail,* 30 October 1958.

50 Johnston, op. cit., p. 277.

51 Informants 13 and 14.

52 Informant 19.

53 30 October 1958.

54 Letter, Minister to Commissioner, 25 September 1959.

55 28 March 1958.

56 Memo, Sub-Inspector CIB to Commissioner, 12 February 1959.

57 General Secretary Queensland Police Union of Employees, to Commissioner, 8 December 1958.

58 17 February 1959.

59 Letter to Minister for Labour and Industry, 2 October 1959.

60 Comment for Under Secretary, letter, Bischof to Minister, Labour and Industry, 19 January 1960.

61 Letter, General Secretary to Commissioner, 12 December 1961.

62 Memo, Boyle to Det. Snr. Sgt. CIB, 23 July 1962.

63 Letter, 26 June 1963.

64 Letter, Bischof to Minister, 26 September 1963.

65 Informant 45.

66 Letter, Herbert to Pizzey, 4 September 1963; Cabinet Submission, 6 August 1964.

67 Letter, 3 June 1964.

68 Queensland Parliamentary Debates, vol. 239, 1964, pp. 1946–1947.

69 Ibid., pp. 1946–2221.

70 Report of the Commissioner of Police (Brisbane, 1965), p. 3; Queensland Police Department, 'Policewomen sworn-in …', n.d.

71 Memo, Boyle to Det. Snr. Sgt. CIB, 22 February 1966.

72 Informant 15; Women Police, Qld Police Union submission to Qld Industrial Court, 1955, p. 3.

73 Informants 46 and 37.

74 Informant 9, also 36.

75 Informant 24.

76 Informant 24.

77 Letter, General Secretary to Bauer, 4 December 1969.

78 Commissioners' Correspondence, December 1969.

79 Letter, Commissioner to Minister, 29 May 1970.

80 Letter, Commissioner to Minister, 29 May 1970; Queensland Government Gazette, 1970, 13 June, p. 982.

81 Queensland Police Journal, 1970, October, p. 8.

82 Ibid.

83 Conference Minutes, 1970, pp. 34–35.

84 The 1970 Plaint for Variation of Police Award — State.

85 Queensland Police Journal, 1970, October, pp. 3, 8–10.

86 Ibid., 1970, September, p. 14.

87 Queensland Government Industrial Gazette, 12 September 1970, p. 29.

88 R. Whitrod, 1988, September, Some Problems of Police Ethics, *Canberra Bulletin of Public Administration*, 56, pp. 38–41.

89 Toscano, 1977, Survey of Policewomen in the Queensland Police Force, Brisbane.

90 Informant 1.

91 *Commissioner's Newsletter*, 1972–76, passim.

92 Informant 1.

93 Queensland Police Service, Personnel Statistics, 1926–78.

94 Informant 9.

95 Letter, Commissioner to Under Secretary Department of Works, 1 November 1972.

96 Memo, Inspector Byles to Superintendent Brisbane Region, 2 December 1973.

97 Letters, Constable P.W.K Weller to Inspector Gold Coast District 8 March 1971; Inspector Ingram to Commissioner, 9 March 1971.

98 Queensland Parliamentary Debates, 26 October, 1971, pp. 1474–1475.

99 Memo, 7 December 1971.

100 Letter, Acting Commissioner Martens to Under Secretary, Department of Works, 18 March 1974.

101 Memo, R. Redmond to CIB, 20 December 1973; Informant 37.

102 Courier Mail, 17 November 1971.

103 Telegraph, 16 November 1971.

104 Informant 1.

105 Ibid.

106 Informant 2.

107 Informant 3.

108 Ibid.

109 Commissioner's Newsletter, passim.

110 Informant 6.

111 Letter, General Secretary, QPU, to Commissioner, 14 September 1970.

112 Letter; General Secretary QPU to Whitrod, 5 May 1976; General Secretary QPU to Minister, 23 March 1976.

113 Deputation by Executive, QPU, to Commissioner, 13 October (1972), pp. 3-4.

114 Commissioners' Correspondence, September to December 1973.

115 *Sunday Sun*, 11 June 1972.

116 *Queensland Police Journal*, June 1972, pp. 9, 11.

117 Informant 2.

118 Informant 2.

119 *Sunday Sun*, 15 July 1973, p. 3.

120 Informant 2.

121 Informant 4.

122 Informant 1.

123 Notes, Commissioners' Conference, Darwin, June 1976.

124 *The Courier-Mail*, 9 February 1974.

125 Johnston, *The Long Blue Line: A History of the Queensland Police*, pp. 284–285.

126 Informant 4.

127 P. Dickie, 1989, *The Road to Fitzgerald and Beyond*, University of Queensland Press, Brisbane; G. Fitzgerald, 1989, *Report of a Commission of Inquiry Pursuant to Orders in Council*, Goprint, Brisbane.

128 Notes, Commissioners' Conference 1976, 1989.

129 Letter, Minister Camm to Mr Gibbs, 26 June 1978; *Past and Present Policewomen's Association of Queensland Magazine* 2(3 1986, p. 5; Informants 7, 10.

130 Prenzler, 1994, op. cit., p. 45.

131 Toscano, op. cit.

132 E.g., *Sunday Sun*, 2 December 1973; *Queensland Police Journal*, 1971, May, p. 36, July, p. 2.

133 Informants 8 and 38.

134 Informant 24.

135 Lewis, Diaries, 12 September 1977.

136 Lewis, Diaries, 14 November 1977.

137 Informant 5.

138 Criminal Justice Commission, 1994, *Report by the Honourable RH Matthews QC on his investigation into the allegations of Lorrelle Anne Saunders concerning the circumstances surrounding her being charged with criminal offences in 1982, and related matters*, Vols. 1 and 2, Brisbane, p. 70.

139 Informant 1.

140 Johnston, op. cit., p. 285.

141 Informant 8.

142 Courier Mail, 4 June 1993, p. 3.

143 Informant 2.

144 Informant 2.

145 Lewis, Diaries, 5 October 1977, 23 December 1977, 24 March 1978, 27 June 1978, 12 July 1978.

146 Informant 6.

147 *The Role and Status of Women in the Queensland Police Force*, n.d., Queensland Police, Brisbane.

148 Informant 4.

149 Informants 7 and 24.

150 *The Telegraph*, 10 March 1982.

151 Lewis, Diaries, 17 December 1976.

152 Informant 6.

153 Past and Present Policewomen's Association of Queensland, 1989, *Submission to Commission of Inquiry into Possible Activities and Associated Police*, Brisbane, p. 7; *The Courier-Mail*, 22 May 1987; *Daily Sun*, 22 June 1987.

154 Informant 6.

155 Informant 7.

156 Informant 6.

157 Informant 6.

158 Informant 4.

159 Informant 6.

160 The *Courier-Mail*, 24 December 1994, p. 7.

161 Commissioners' Correspondence (1987), passim.

162 Memo, Assistant Commissioner Braithwaite to Acting Commissioner, 15 February 1988; Letter, Redmond to Assistant Commissioner Personnel, 31 October 1988; Commissioners' Correspondence November, 1987, passim.

163 Memo, Acting Inspector Sgroi to Superintendent, Legal Section, 17 October 1989.

164 Past and Present Policewomen's Association of Queensland, op. cit.

165 Fitzgerald, op cit., p. 246.

166 Ibid., p. 246.

167 R. Lewis, 1994, *Recruitment of Target Group Members to the Queensland Police*, Queensland Police, Brisbane, p. 3.

168 Queensland Police Service, 1993, *Equal Employment Opportunity Plan 1993/94 and Evaluation Report 1992/3*, Brisbane, p. 82.

169 Prenzler, op. cit., p. 87.

170 Statistical Co-ordination Unit, 1993, Queensland Police Service, Brisbane.

171 Informant 2.

Chapter 4

1 M. Thornton, 1990, *The Liberal Promise*, Oxford University Press, Melbourne; M. Thornton, 2001, EEO in a Neo-liberal Climate, *Journal of Interdisciplinary Gender Studies*, 6(1), 77–104.

2 C. Nixon, 1994, 'The Role of Women in Policing', in D. Moore and R. Wettenhall (Eds.) *Keeping the Peace: Police Accountability and Oversight* (pp. 74–77), University of Canberra and the Royal Institute of Public Administration Australia, Canberra, p. 75.

3 T. Prenzler and J. Drew, 2013, Women Police in Post-Fitzgerald Queensland: A 20 Year Review, *Australian Journal of Public Administration*, 72(4), 459–472.

4 Queensland Police Service, 1993, *Equal Employment Opportunity Plan 1993/94 and Evaluation Report 1992/93*, Brisbane, pp. 47, 52, 68, 85.

5 Prenzler and Drew, op. cit.

6 T. Prenzler, 2004, Gender Discrimination and Regulatory Behaviour: A Case Study in Policing, *International Journal of Police Science and Management*, 6(3), 171–182, pp. 174 and 176.

7 T. Prenzler, 1995, Equal Employment Opportunity and Policewomen in Australia, *Australian and New Zealand Journal of Criminology*, 28(3), 258–277.

8 Victoria Police, 1990, *The Impact of Equal Opportunity on Policing in Victoria*, Melbourne.

9 T. Prenzler and H. Hayes, 2000, Measuring Progress in Gender Equity in Australian Policing, *Current Issues in Criminal Justice*, 12(1), 20–38.

10 Ibid, p. 24.

11 Ibid, p. 25.

12 Ibid, p. 31.

13 Ibid, p. 32.

14 Ibid, p. 34.

15 Ibid.

16 Ibid.

17 Ibid, pp. 35–36.

18 Federation of Community Legal Centres Victoria, 1993, *Brute Force: The Need for Affirmative Action in the Victorian Police Force*, Melbourne, pp. 3–4.

19 Ibid, p. 4.

20 Federation of Community Legal Centres Victoria (1999) Brute Force II: The Continuing Need for Affirmative Action in the Victorian Police Force, Melbourne.

21 T. Prenzler, 2004, Interview with Christine Nixon: Australia's First Female Police Chief, *Police Practice and Research: An International Journal,* 5(4), 301–315; pp. 308–309.

22 Prenzler, 1994, op. cit., p. 65.

23 Prenzler, 1995, op. cit.

24 J. Sutton, 1996, *Survey of New South Wales Policewomen.* Paper presented to the First Australasian Women in Policing Conference, Sydney, 29–31 July.

25 Ibid, pp. 11–12.

26 Ibid, p. 16.

27 M. Circelli, 1998, What are the Problems and Issues Facing Women in Policing? *The Journal for Women and Policing,* No. 1, p. 28.

28 N. Boni and M. Circelli, 2002, *Contemporary Issues Facing Women in Policing,* Australasian Centre for Policing Research, Adelaide.

29 Ibid, p. 84.

30 Ibid, p. 32.

31 K. Adams, 2001, *Women in Senior Police Management,* Australasian Centre for Policing Research, Adelaide.

32 Ibid, p. 29.

33 Ibid, p. 31.

34 Ibid, pp. v-vi.

35 Prenzler, 2004, op. cit.

36 T. Prenzler, 1996, 'Rebuilding the Walls? The Impact of Police Pre-entry Physical Ability Tests on Female Applicants', *Current Issues in Criminal Justice,* 7(3), 314–324.

37 Federation of Community Legal Centres Victoria, 1999, op. cit., p. 27.

38 N. Sikora, 3 June 1998, Five years lost to abuse, *Herald Sun,* p. 14.

39 N. Sikora, 29 May 2000, Police delay payout, *Herald Sun,* p. 10.

40 Flannery v. O'Sullivan (No.1) (Queensland Anti-Discrimination Tribunal, 1993), pp. 1–15.

41 Prenzler and Drew, op. cit.

42 In *The Courier-Mail,* 19 January 1993, p. 5.

43 In *Sunday Mail,* 24 January 1993, p. 62.

44 Prenzler and Drew, op. cit., p. 465.

45 Prenzler, 1994, op. cit.

46 Tasmania Police, 1997, *Annual Report 1996/97,* Hobart, p. 100.

47 1998, November 21, p. 6.

48 Ibid.

49 E. Whinnett, 6 May 2000, 'The Girls in Blue', *Hobart Mercury*, p. 31.

50 *Sunday Examiner*, 24 June 2001, p 22.

51 C. Niland, 1996, *The Impact of Police Culture on Women and their Performance in Policing.* Paper presented at the First Australasian Women in Policing Conference, Sydney, 29–31 July.

52 Ibid, pp. 7–8

53 M. Palmer, 1996, *Where to From Here?* Paper presented at the First Australasian Women in Policing Conference, Sydney, 29–31 July

54 J. Bradley, 1996, *AFP Strategies to Implement Equity and Diversity Objectives.* Paper presented at the First Australasian Women in Policing Conference, Sydney, 29–31 July

Chapter 5

1 The Western Australian Police Service and the University of Western Australia, 2003, *SPIRT Project: Report to the Commissioner of Police: Redressing the Gendered Workplace Culture of Policing*, Perth, p. 35.

2 H. Nott, 10 December 2003, 'WA — Policewomen subject to systemic discrimination — report'. Australian Associated Press General News.

3 A. Mullany, 16 November 2013, 'New campaign to attract more female, multiculural police', *PerthNow*. Retrieved from http://www.perthnow.com.au/news/western-australia/new-campaign-to-attract-more-female-multicultural-police/story-fnhocxo3-1226761622584

4 *The Journal for Women and Policing*, 1998, No. 1, p. 11.

5 K. Towers, 5 February 1999, 'Promise of uniform rights', *The Australian*, p. 3.

6 Ibid.

7 D. Farrant, 11 December 1999, *The Age*, p. 18.

8 L. Porter, 3 August 2003, 'Police Pay Out $1m for Bullies', *Sunday Age*, p. 1.

9 Ibid.

10 Australian Broadcasting Corporation (ABC) News, 13 November 2014, Victoria Police Review to Examine Sexual Harassment, Predatory Behaviour (http://www.abc.net.au/news/2014-11-13/review-ordered-into-sexual-harassment-within-victoria-police/5887448).

11 T. Prenzler, J. Fleming, & A. King, 2010, Gender Equity in Australian and New Zealand Policing: A Five Year Review, *International Journal of Police Science and Management*, 12(4), 584–595.

12 Ibid, p. 588.

13 Ibid, p. 589.

14 Ibid, p. 590.

15 Ibid, p. 590.

16 Ibid, p. 592.

17 New South Wales Police Force, *Annual Report 2013–14*, p. 80.

18 Australian Institute of Criminology. Retrieved from http://www.aic.gov.au/statistics/criminaljustice/police_services.html
Note: The Northern Territory includes Aboriginal Community Police Officers (ACPOs) and auxiliary officers.

19 Ibid

20 Australian Bureau of Statistics, 2015, supplied to author.

21 Nixon & Chandler, op. cit.

22 M. Chulov, 28–9 September 2002, 'The Force is with Her: The Rise and Rise of Australia's First Female Police Chief', *The Weekend Australian Magazine*, pp. 13–15.

23 Nixon & Chandler, op. cit., p. 328.

24 Ibid.

25 *The Journal for Women and Policing*, 1998, No. 1, p. 2.

26 Ibid, p. 1.

27 Australasian Council for Women and Policing (http://www. acwap.com.au/about-us/)

28 Australasian Council for Women and Policing (http://www. acwap.com.au/management-committee/)

Postscript

1 Appier, op. cit., p. 5; F. Heidensohn, 1992, *Women in Control? The Role of Women in Law Enforcement*, Clarendon Press, Oxford.

2 Appier, op. cit.

3 Ibid.

4 Stella, op. cit., p. vi.

5 Appier, op. cit., p. 33.

6 Informants 13 and 14, see also *The Courier-Mail*, 5 December 1956.

7 J. Hunt, 1990, 'The Logic of Sexism Among Police, Women and Criminal Justice', *1*(2), 3–30; see also J. Balkin, 1988, 'Why Policemen Don't Like Policewomen', *Journal of Police Science and Administration*, *16*(1), 29–38.

8 Ibid, Hunt.

9 See P. Lunneborg, 1989, *Women Police Officers: Current Career Profile*, Charles C. Thomas, Springfield IL.

10 See K. Lonsway et al., 2002, *Men, Women, and Excessive Force: A Tale of Two Genders*, National Center for Women and Policing, Beverly Hills, CA: National Centre for Women and Policing; L. Porter and T. Prenzler (forthcoming). *Police Officer Gender and Excessive Force Complaints: An Australian Study*, Policing and Society.

11 For example, T. Prenzler, 1997, 'A Problem Oriented Approach to Preventing Sex Discrimination in Police Recruitment', *Crime Prevention Studies*, *7*, 207–222; T. Prenzler and G. Sinclair, 2013, 'The Status of Women Police Officers: An International Review', *International Journal of Law, Crime and Justice*, *41*(2), 115–131.

12 M. Bastick, 2014, *Integrating Gender into Internal Police Oversight*, DCAF (Democratic Control of Armed Forces), Organisation for Security and Cooperation in Europe, Geneva.

9 781922 117601